Welcome to
your new home!
Hope you love it
in Rosemoor as much as
do.

MY HOUSEFUL OF HINTS

How to Solve Problems
at Home and Away

Best Regards,

Doris B. Gill

Also by Doris B. Gill

MY HOUSE TO YOURS
How to Look Younger, Feel Better,
& Live a Happier Life

Published by Crab Cove Books

If you cannot find our books in your book store, you may order direct from Crab Cove Books. Just send us the book's title, author, and ISBN number (if you know it) and a check or money order for the retail price plus $1.50 for shipping and handling, or $11.45 total. Californians add appropriate tax.

Mail to:
    Crab Cove Books
    P.O. Box 2015
    Walnut Creek, CA 94595
    Phone: (510) 945-0854

Crab Cove Books are available at special discounts when purchased in bulk quantities, for organizations, and corporations. Please call us about customized imprints, excerpts, or any special requirements you may have.

MY HOUSEFUL OF HINTS

How to Solve Problems at Home and Away

Doris B. Gill

Crab Cove Books

For information write or call:

Crab Cove Books
P.O. Box 2015
Walnut Creek, CA 94595
Phone: (510)945-0854

Typography by Cragmont Publications, Oakland, CA

Line Drawings by Ron Camara, Qualitype, Oakland, CA

First Printing 1989
Second Printing 1997

Printed in The United States of America

Library of Congress Catalog Card Number: 89-91761

ISBN 0-9618693-6-4

Table of Contents

I would like to extend my sincere appreciation to Don Johnson, Eileen Harry, Charlotte Smith, and Howard Hipkins for their extensive efforts in editing, making suggestions, and their tremendous support.

Thanks and my gratitude for the great tips provided by:

Jane Macdonald
Toni Rivera
Margaret Horton

Preface

In my first book, *My House To Yours*, the household hints in the chapter "Do Your House A Favor," proved to be very popular. When the book first came out, a national tabloid bought second rights for the cleaning tips.

Because of this popularity, I decided to devote an entire book to the subject. Some of the original hints are included in this book, as well as many, many new ones.

Much thought has gone into the type of hints included. For instance, in the chapter "In The Kitchen," only healthy foods and drinks were considered. You will not find tips about frying, rich pastries, granulated sugar, bacon, pork, solid shortening, liquor, carbonated beverages, or cooking with aluminum foil.

The hints are from various sources. Some are handed down from my French Grandmother, others are from my own experience gained while raising my four children, and also as a working, single parent. Many of my friends have graciously contributed their favorite, money saving, short cuts.

Whether you are an established homemaker, or just starting out, I hope you enjoy this book and find it a practical guide in, and around your home, and even further afield.

Sips of Life

A drop of rain
A ray of sun
A shady glen
A flake of snow
A breath of wind
A kiss of love
A look of hope
A touch of care
A fleeting smile
A helpful hint
Sips of life

CHAPTER 1

In the Kitchen

FOOD FOR THOUGHT

General

Appetizers will look very appealing if you use pretzel sticks in place of cocktail toothpicks. People will think you are very creative. The pretzel will penetrate the food easily, if first, you make a hole with a skewer or paring knife. But be kind to your guests (and yourself), use pretzel sticks with reduced salt. An added bonus: there is only one calorie per pretzel stick.

Heat tea water quickly in the microwave oven or on the stove top. Boil only ½ to ¾ cup of water. After steeping, add cold water. You will take less time and electricity and the drink will be just right to drink without cooling.

Pot luck dinners—If you contribute to a party get-together, let the guests know it is your dish. Place a card in front of, or attached to your contributing container. Print what it is and your name. Someone may want the recipe or want to say "thanks."

Punch base—Always start with tea as a base, then add your favorite fruit juices, and mineral water. Use white grape juice for sweetness and lemon for a zingy taste.

Minor burns can be relieved simply. Run the burned area under cold water until it stops hurting (about one minute). If this is not practical, apply a clean, cold cloth and ice to the burn. Then pour white or cider vinegar on a clean cloth or white paper napkin and wrap it around the area. Leave it in place for 10 or 15 minutes, or until the burn feels relieved. This will help prevent blistering. If the burn is serious, see a doctor.

Measuring dry herbs—One teaspoon of dried herbs is equivalent to one tablespoon of fresh herbs.

Hard brown sugar—Transfer the sugar from the original box to a round, soft, plastic container. If the sugar becomes hard, lay the container on its side and roll across the counter top until the sugar is loose. If it is still too hard, grate it with a cheese grater.

Slow running catsup—Insert a straw in and out of the bottle a few times. This will provide air on which the sauce can ride.

Make your own catsup—To one 8 oz. can of tomato sauce, add 1/3 cup of raw honey, a dash of salt, and a dash of allspice.

No muscle man around to open tightly capped bottles or jars?—Take your choice with one of these easy solutions. Run hot water over the lid; the hot temperature makes the lid expand. If it is a glass container that has been refrigerated, wait at least five minutes after removing it from the refrigerator to prevent breakage. Now try turning the lid with a damp cloth. This should give you more leverage. If this fails to budge the lid, place a wide rubber band around it before turning. Another method is to put on a rubber glove. This should give you a good grip on things. If every other method fails, use large pliers.

Want to cut down on salt?—Try this devious trick. Cover all the salt shaker holes, except two, with transparent tape. Scratch across the tape with your thumb nail to provide a good seal and reduce the evidence. You and your family will reap the benefits of a reduced salt diet and they may not notice the difference. Using the tape will also help prevent accidental over-seasoning.

Reduce salt with Tamari—Tamari is Japanese soy sauce made from naturally fermented beans. Depending on the brand, it not only has less salt, but may be free of wheat as well.

Store extra ice cubes in paper bags in your freezer when you are making extra ice. They will not stick together.

Use clear plastic produce bags to protect food stored in coverless bowls or jars. Twist the bag tightly around the container and fasten with a wire clip. Plastic wrap is expensive and does not always adhere to some materials. Besides, the produce bags are free and you are doing your part by recycling them.

Crackers will stay fresh longer if you store them in your oven drawer. Once a divided packet has been opened, wrap it in plastic before returning it to the box. Opened crackers can also be stored in tightly closed tins.

Substitute peanut butter on morning toast in place of butter. It is more nutritious than the dairy spread and is a nice change. You can also add other things to the peanut butter such as sliced bananas or cinnamon and honey.

Waffles in a jiffy—When preparing waffle batter, double the normal recipe. Cook it all and store the leftovers. After cooling, break into fours, place in plastic bags and store in the freezer. Now you can have this tasty treat ready, even on a weekday morning without spending a lot of money. Simply remove some from the freezer and pop them into the toaster.

Prepare vitamins in advance—If you take more than a few supplements, prepare them for a week or more at one time, instead of meting them out each busy morning. Save small containers with tightly fitting lids. Miniature jelly glasses, prescription drug plastic bottles, and pimiento jars all make good storage containers. Wash and dry the bottles thoroughly before filling. If the vitamins are prepared in advance, it may encourage you to take them regularly, even when you are in a hurry.

When travelling, put the vitamins in plastic sandwich bags. Place all the bags in a larger bag, and label them with the name of each member of the family.

Eggs

Keep hard boiled eggs from cracking while they are cooking. Carefully puncture the small end of the shell with a pin or tack before placing it in the water. This will also make peeling easier.

When hard boiled eggs are undercooked try this: Pierce with a fork after peeling and place in the microwave oven in a covered dish. Cook at the half power setting for about 10 seconds or for 5 second on full power. Check the doneness and if it is still under cooked, repeat until it is just the way you like it.

Hard boiled eggs will peel easily if you do this first: gently roll them between your hands or across the kitchen counter until they are cracked, then peel beginning with the air pocket end.

Which egg is hard boiled?—If you cannot tell which is which, simply spin the egg. If it spins smoothly, it is hard cooked, if it acts like a drunken Humpty Dumpty and wobbles, you know it is fresh. The fresh egg's liquid is sloshing inside.

Hard boiled egg shells can be removed easily if you place the eggs in water *after* the water has started to boil. When they have finished cooking, remove from the heat immediately and immerse in cold water until cool.

Slice hard boiled eggs cleanly—Dip the knife in water before each stroke. The yolk will not stick to the knife.

Extra yolks—Consider two yolks as one egg in a recipe.

Next time you make scrambled eggs try adding water as you beat the eggs. Add one tablespoon of water for each egg. They will be lighter than if you use milk and go farther than if you add nothing.

Separate egg whites from yolks by breaking them into a funnel. The white will pass through and the yolk will remain.

For light, fluffy waffles separate the egg whites from the yolks. Add the beaten yolks to the batter, but save the whites. Place them in a small mixing bowl and beat them until stiff peaks form. When the batter is completely mixed, carefully fold in the whites.

Dairy Products

Grate soft cheese easily by putting it in the freezer for 10 or 15 minutes before grating.

Liven up grilled cheese sandwiches—Spread the bread with mayonnaise instead of butter or margarine. It goes on easily and gives the sandwich a great flavor.

Cut calories on toasted cheese sandwiches— Place the cheese directly on plain bread and broil, open-faced. The edges of the bread will be crispy. If you prefer the entire slice to be crisp, toast the bread slightly before applying the cheese.

Cheese will stay moist if you wrap it in a cloth that has been soaked in vinegar and wrung out. Then, place the package in a plastic sack to keep the vinegar odor inside. *Cheese will not dry out* if, after using it, you rub the remaining cut edge with vegetable oil.

Economical and good tasting milk—To make a quart of non-fat dry milk, add ¼ cup of fresh milk. You may use whole milk, 2% milk, or non-fat milk. When it is chilled, it will taste almost like the real thing. Your children may not be able to tell the difference.

Ice cream that is too hard to serve—Peel or cut away the carton and slice the desert with a knife.

Fruits

Sliced bananas will not discolor as quickly, if you cover them with lemon juice. In a fruit salad, the citrus adds a fresh, tangy taste.

Ripe bananas will last a little longer if they are peeled and placed in a covered jar in the refrigerator.

California Fruit Desert—Wash, peel, and cube, cantaloupe, watermelon, pears, apples, bananas, straw-berries, and any other seasonal fruit. Mix and store them in a large bowl. When you are ready to serve din-ner, remove the fruit from the refrigerator. Scoop sher-bert (pineapple, orange, or lime) over the fruit. Leave it at room temperature, unless the weather is extremely warm. It will melt and blend with the fruit. Spoon into serving dishes for a delicious treat.

Freshen shredded coconut by soaking it in milk for a few minutes. Drain thoroughly before using.

Add color to coconut—Place a cup of this shred-ded fruit into a jar and add 3 drops of food coloring. Cover the jar tightly with a lid and shake until the color is evenly distributed.

Ripen hard persimmons, by placing them in a paper bag along with an apple or banana. In a few days they will be *very* soft and ready to eat immediately. De-licious!

For perfect apple or pear butter use a crockpot or slow cooker. Your favorite recipe can be used and the fruit spread will not scorch or stick.

Keep strawberries fresh longer—These delicious

morsels will last longer without becoming moldy, if you keep them uncovered in the refrigerator. Leave them in the original store basket, but remove the plastic lid. Store the basket loosely in a plastic bag that is open at the top or place the basket on a folded paper towel.

When selecting fresh cantaloupe, choose a melon that is light colored, with as little green as possible. Store it at room temperature for a day or two before eating. The melon should be sweet and succulent. Keep an eye on it to make sure it does not become too ripe.

Low calorie summer cooler—Fill an 8 oz. tumbler ⅓ full of cranberry juice (sweetened with white grapes, not sugar) and a squeeze of lemon. Fill the glass with bottled water and ice cubes. Place a lemon slice on the glass lip and it is ready to serve.

Low-cal toast spread—Heat two tablespoons of apple juice or any other juice. Pour it over ½ cup of your favorite dried fruit. Use raisins, apricots, prunes, or other fruit. Perhaps you would like to mix two fruits together. Try dried apples and pears. Add a squeeze of orange or lemon juice for a zingy taste. Chop or grind to a paste and store in your refrigerator.

Low-cal salad dressing—Blend pineapple, orange, and grapefruit in equal parts. Add a squeeze of lemon and honey to taste. Use this fruitful delight on cabbage, seafood, or fruit salads.

Date sugar is a good natural sweetener and may be purchased at most health food stores.

Grains

Oatmeal adds flavor and richness when used as a soup thickener. Add two tablespoons of raw oats to your next potful of soup in place of corn starch. Also use oatmeal to thicken stews. You may even use morning left-over cooked oat cereal.

Out of milk? Try serving morning oatmeal with a spoonful of molasses (to taste), three heaping table-spoons of plain, low fat yogurt, and fruit juice in place of milk. Apple and pineapple is a tasty combination, or try your own favorites. The molasses/yogurt/juice combination is so good, you may prefer it to your usual toppings. It is also helpful for those who are milk-sensitive.

Make rice more nutritious. Save the water from cooking vegetables and store it in a covered container in the freezer. Use it in place of plain water the next time you cook rice. It will add nutrients to the rice and give it more flavor.

Rice will not stick together if you add a teaspoon of lemon juice to the cooking water. One tablespoon of vegetable oil will also keep rice from sticking.

Cooking brown rice properly—Some people think they do not like this nutritious grain, but if it is cooked long enough, it is delicious. Simmer for 45 minutes in a covered pan. Remove from the heat and let it stand for five minutes before serving. (Follow the package instructions to the letter). Now that so many diets include complex carbohydrates, this is a good time to include a rice that has not had most of the value removed. California Brown Rice is an especially good brand. After opening the package, keep the remainder in the freezer. Brown rice does not keep over an extended period. It could become rancid.

Cold cereals have become outrageously expensive. Save money, receive more value, and more nutrition. Buy only the basic cereals such as corn flakes, wheat flake, Rice Crispies, or any other plain, mostly unsweetened cereals which are less costly. Add your own embellishments such as nuts, raisins, and fresh fruit.

Reduce unpopped kernels in popcorn. Store them in the freezer.

For perfect pasta, add one teaspoon of vegetable oil to the water. Add the pasta only after the water is boiling rapidly. Stir once with a wooden spoon. The pasta will not stick together. The oil will also help prevent boil-overs.

From the Oven

Slice baked goods with ease:

Brownies— Cut into squares while they are still hot. This will prevent crumbling or sticking to the knife.

Cakes— After cooling, slice with a knife dipped in hot water. Shake off excess water. The heated knife will encourage a smooth, trim cut. Dental floss can also be used. Wrap tightly around both hands and bring down through the cake. First, mark the top of the cake with a knife, for uniform slices.

Oat bran—Adding oat bran to foods has almost become a fad. Some food producers are cashing in on the popularity of this healthy grain. When considering the use of products containing bran such as cookies, cereals, and muffins, we must ask ourselves: "Is this product really healthy?" Just because a product contains oat bran, does not mean it is good for us. Many cereals, breads and muffins that have added oat bran, still contain ingredients such as sugars, chemicals, and other items you may not want in your diet. Before you purchase these products, read the labels carefully. If you want to know exactly what goes into bran muffins, make your own.

Below is my recipe for OAT FLOWERS. These muffins are named "flowers" because they contain no flour:

OAT FLOWERS

Preheat oven to 400° F.   Makes 12-14 muffins

Mix in a large bowl:

1 ripe banana, mashed   ¼ cup raw sunflower seeds
2 eggs, beaten   (store in freezer)
2 cups oat bran   ¼ cup walnuts
⅓ cup oats   (store in freezer)
1 teaspoon vanilla   2 tablespoons safflower oil
1 tablespoon Rumford   (store in refrigerator)
    baking powder   4 tablespoons (or less) honey
¼ cup raisins   4 tablespoons (or less)
                                  molasses

Mix all ingredients and spoon into muffin tins lined with cupcake papers. Bake for 15-18 minutes. Cool, and place in a plastic bag, and store in the freezer. Heat as needed in the microwave oven for about 15 seconds.

If you worry about baking powder containing sodium aluminum sulphate, you can now buy this leavening agent with only these ingredients: calcium acid phosphate, bicarbonate of soda, and corn starch. It works well, is double acting, and available at health food stores. The brand name is Rumford. If you cannot find it, write to Rumford Company, Dept. D, 900 Wabash Avenue, Terre Haute, Indiana 47801

Before reheating pizza brush it with vegetable oil. It will be more moist.

Poultry, Meat, & Fish

Defrosting chicken—Because of the rapid deteri-
oration of uncooked chicken, the temperature should
never drop below 30 degrees F. To be safe, defrost in the
microwave oven or refrigerator.

Freezing chicken—To extend the freezer life, do
not freeze chicken in its original packaging. Remove
from the package and wash in cool water with one tablespoon of salt. Rinse in clear water and pat dry with
paper towels and place in a zip-lock bag before freezing.
When you finish, be sure to wash all utensils in hot
soapy water to prevent bacteria contamination.

Tenderize chicken and other fowl by rubbing the
inside and outside of the bird with lemon juice before
cooking. Do this after thoroughly washing.

Golden brown chicken—Put ½ cup of powdered
milk in a bag with poultry pieces and shake. Use this
instead of flour, it is great for people who are allergic to
wheat.

More poultry stuffing than bird?—Place the
extra dressing in an oiled baking dish along with the
neck, giblets, and gizzards (for flavor). Cover and bake
with the bird.

Remove chicken skin easily by using a clean dish
cloth. The cloth will enable you to get a better grip on
the skin.

Applying barbecue sauce is a snap if you use a
small, new paint brush. The sauce will go on easily and
evenly. Use it for outdoor cooking or oven cooking.

Turkey hamburger is 93% fat free. Use it in place
of beef when it is in a sauce (such as in Spanish rice or
tamale pie). When you brown the turkey hamburger,
cook it very slowly. It browns quickly, so it is not necessary to "fry" it. Because it is so lean, you may find it

necessary to add a small amount of vegetable oil to the cooking pan.

Baked turkey drumsticks and dressing make a delicious and economical meal that can be enjoyed any time of year. Start with two legs (ask the meat cutter to remove the skin). Place the legs in a heavy baking pan, which has been rubbed with vegetable oil. In a large bowl add 1 cup chopped celery (include the leaves), 1 cup chopped onions, 1 cup sliced carrots, 2 cups bread cubes (dried), 1 beaten egg and ¼ teaspoon sage. Add 1 cup of liquid, water or cold broth to soften the bread. Mix and spoon the mixture over the legs. Bake in a covered pan at 300 degrees for about four hours, or until tender. Serve with cranberry sauce and a tossed salad. The turkey will serve four nicely with leftovers. The drumstick bones can be saved for soup stock. (Watch carefully for those splintery bones).

Delicious hamburger st-r-r-r-etcher—Add a new taste to burgers. Wash one medium potato for each pound of meat. Peeling is not necessary, there is nourishment in the skin. Now, grate, or grind the potato and add to the ground round before making the patties. Grill, or broil in the usual manner. The burgers will be crispy and will make more servings.

Preparing hamburger for browning—Place the meat in a large bowl and use a potato masher to separate before cooking.

Low-cal hamburger—Always buy the leanest ground beef. After browning, drain in a colander or strainer. Splash with water and drain before returning it to the pan.

Give meat loaf and meat balls a tasty new flavor by adding a teaspoon of dry mustard when mixing the raw meat.

Basic, browned beef in a hurry—Brown a few

pounds at one time. Divide into serving-size packages and freeze. It will be just a thaw away from many hamburger dishes. P.S.—Be sure to drain off the fat before storing.

Fish that has been frozen will taste fresher if you dip it in milk before cooking.

Tuna will always taste good if you buy Albacore. It is never bitter. Use the water-packed type for fewer calories.

Poor man's lobster, or Monk fish, can really taste like its sophisticated and expensive cousin, the lobster. Use this simple method when preparing. Cover the fish with water, add ½ teaspoon of salt and simmer slowly with a lid on the pot. Boil gently until tender (15-20 minutes) depending on the size of the fish. It is done when a fork goes through it easily. Now the secret of success: When the fish is cooked it will be white, all except for a purplish-brown membrane which runs through one end. Remove this membrane by cutting the fish away from it and throw it away. Serve the fish with melted butter, a pinch of garlic powder, and lemon. You will enjoy this lobster-like flavor at a fraction of the cost of the real thing.

Add a little jazz to your seafood Louis—Horseradish will liven up Thousand Island dressing. Start with a very small amount of horseradish (½ teaspoon) and increase until it satisfies your taste. It will enhance the shrimp or crab. (This tip was from an ex-New York chef now residing in California.)

Reduce smoke and splatters when broiling— Place stale bread in the broiler tray. The bread will absorb the grease which helps prevent it from becoming so hot.

Vinegar is an effective meat tenderizer—When stewing meat, add one tablespoon of vinegar to the cooking water. When roasting meat, pour one tablespoon of vinegar over the roast. Baste often. Tough meat and poultry can be tenderized by soaking in a marinade of vinegar, water, and vegetable oil overnight. Use one half cup vinegar, one half cup water, and two tablespoons of vegetable oil. Mix well and pour over the meat or poultry. Cover and store in the refrigerator overnight.

Marinate in a plastic bag and avoid the mess— Place a plastic bag in a bowl large enough to hold the contents to be marinated. After the pieces of poultry or meat are placed in the bag, add your favorite sauce. Twist the bag securely closed and carefully turn over until the sauce is evenly distributed. Keep it in the refrigerator; turn over at least twice during the soaking period.

Vegetables

Avocados will discolor less, if you leave the seed in place. This works even if the avocado is peeled.

Oh, oh too much salt?—Add a potato to dishes such as stews or other vegetables that are too salty. The potato will absorb the excess salt and may be discarded before serving.

Beets will stay bright and taste better if you add a teaspoon of fresh lemon to the cooking water.

Beets will practically pop out of their skins if, after steaming, they are splashed with cold water.

Wilted celery and lettuce will perk up quickly if you place them in ice water to which several slices of raw potato have been added. Remember that the water will rob the vegetables of some of their nutrients, so do not leave them in the water any longer than necessary. Save the water for cooking or for plant watering.

Corn on the cob will stay moist and unbruised if you buy it unshucked.

Fruits and vegetables will stay fresh longer if you control the moisture in your refrigerator. Line your crisper with paper towels, which will help absorb much of the excess moisture.

Peeling garlic—Press the clove with the flat side of a knife. It will split the outer skin, making peeling easy.

1⁄8 teaspoon of garlic powder equals one small garlic clove.

Remove garlic or onion odor from hands—Rub a stainless steel utensil with your hands under running water. Very simple and very effective. Another method is to peel onions first, then prepare celery.

Onion juice—Cut the onion in half and use your orange juice squeezer to extract the liquid.

Store leftover raw Bermuda onions in a glass jar with a tightly fitting lid. They will last longer and retain their fresh flavor.

Keep onions in the refrigerator—This will reduce tears (the boo-hoo kind) during peeling.

Stemmed vegetables, such as broccoli or cauliflower will cook quickly if you cut a 1⁄4 inch cross at the end of the stem.

Steaming alarm—When steaming vegetables, add a few marbles to the cooking water. If the water boils away, the marbles will alert you when they rattle in the bottom of the empty pan.

A cone-shaped, microwave popcorn popper can double as a very efficient vegetable steamer. Just add two tablespoons of water and cook in the usual way.

Store fresh parsley in a covered jar in the refrigerator. It will stay fresh and crisp longer.

Cut parsley for salad easily—Wash under running water, shake, and snip with a pair of scissors.

Some children and adults do not like the texture of eggs in potato salad—If you have this problem, but would like to know the children are getting the nutritious eggs, try this:

Mash the hard boiled eggs in a small mixing bowl. Add the mayonnaise you plan to use in your salad and a small amount of mustard (approximately ¼ teaspoon to a quart of salad). Mix together and blend into the potatoes and other ingredients. Your salad will be quite yellow and taste delicious as the "sauce" permeates the potatoes. Your family will receive all the benefits of the eggs, without even knowing it. We liked this method so much that we continued to do it even when the children grew older. There were always many compliments from the diners.

Add a little sunshine to a winter salad with this reduced calorie dressing:

> 1 cup orange juice
> 1 tablespoon toasted sesame seeds
> 3 tablespoons natural vinegar
> 1 tablespoon raw honey
> ⅓ cup safflower oil
> ½ teaspoon dill weed
> ½ teaspoon dry mustard
> 1 clove garlic, chopped or minced

Combine all ingredients in a pint jar with a tightly fitting lid. Store in the refrigerator and shake before using. It is good on any leafy winter salad.

Save pea pods and celery tops to use for soup flavoring. Store in air-tight plastic bags in the freezer until needed.

Save leftover vegetables for that next batch of

soup—Store them in the freezer until needed.

Soup is nutritious, fat is not—After you prepare stock, cool and skim the fat that has congealed on top. Store in the refrigerator. A tablespoon of lecithin granules can also be added when reheating. It will gobble up any fat you may have missed. Lecithin can be purchased at most health food stores and should be refrigerated.

Vegetable soup will have more flavor if you add V-8 juice in place of 1 cup of water when adding the vegetables to the pot.

Give stews, soups, and dressings more flavor— Saute onions, celery and carrots before adding to the recipe. Cook them in a skillet with enough vegetable oil to cover the bottom of the pan and cook at a *very* low temperature. Remove from the pan when they are transparent, not fully cooked. Do not let the oil get too hot.

Oatmeal is a good soup thickener—Add a couple of tablespoons to any soup that is too thin.

A baked potato in a jiffy—If you like a spud with a crispy skin, but do not have enough time to bake it in a conventional oven, try this method: Cook the potato in the microwave in a covered dish, with two tablespoons of water. Cook each potato for about 4 minutes and then turn it over and cook for another 3 or 4 minutes, depending on the size of the potato and the power of your microwave oven. When the potato is almost done (pierce it with a fork) and place it in a hot (450 degree) oven for about five minutes or until crispy.

An even faster method, is to slice the potato lengthwise before putting it in the oven. It will cook in a shorter time and have a crispy top. If you prefer not to have a crispy crust, bake the potato with the flat side down.

Now that you have the potato ready, how about a topping?

Low calorie baked potato topping—Spoon non-fat, plain yogurt, lemon juice, and chives over baked potatoes for a tasty treat.

Cream cheese has less calories than butter, try it for a diet topping.

Stretching Chinese food left-overs—Chinese food is great the next day for lunch or dinner. However, there may not be enough to go around. To stretch those Chinese delights, such as fried rice, chow mein, or meat and poultry dishes, simply add vegetables. Fresh, frozen, or leftovers will all work well. Mixed vegetables, spinach, peas, cabbage, tomatoes, green peppers, Bermuda or green onions, and carrots are a few good examples. Steam the vegetables and remove them from the steamer before they are thoroughly done, add to the Chinese food before heating so that the flavor will enhance the dish. Chop green onions for a tasty garnish and sprinkle over the top of the dish before serving. Have steamed rice on the side and for dessert, some fresh fruit, like tangerines or orange slice and yogurt, and of course, fortune cookies. The entire family should enjoy it.

Tomatoes will last longer in your refrigerator if you leave the stems in place. This seems to nourish the tomatoes.

Ripen tomatoes by storing them on top of the refrigerator. The warmth from the motor will hasten the ripening process.

Low-cal spread or dip for vegetables, sandwiches, and crackers:

Mix in the blender:

        1 cup cottage cheese (low fat)

        1 clove garlic

        1 teaspoon chives

        1/8 teaspoon paprika

Store in a covered container in the refrigerator. Serve when chilled.

If children dislike vegetables, undercook them. Kids usually like the texture better and they will reap the extra benefit of receiving more nutrients. Steaming is best for preserving the flavor and goodness of vegetables.

CLEANING UP

Kitchen appliances will sparkle if you clean them with a solution of baking soda and water. Add four tablespoons to a quart of water and wipe the surface, rinse, and dry. If there are stubborn stains simply sprinkle a little baking soda on a cloth or sponge and rub. The baking soda will not scratch the finish and will remove most kitchen grime.

Clean the range exhaust filter by running it through your automatic dishwasher.

Clean oven racks by carefully placing them in the bathtub or wash tray. Cover with hot water and Spic & Span. Soak overnight. All the black residue should be gone.

When food is spilled in a hot oven, sprinkle salt on the area. When the oven is cool, brush off the residue and wipe with a damp cloth.

Water spots on stainless steel appliances and sinks can be removed with rubbing alcohol.

White appliances that have yellowed may be restored to their original whiteness with a solution of borax and water. Mix ½ cup of borax in two quarts of warm water and wipe the surface. Rinse and dry.

Cleaning the garbage disposal—Pour one cup of vinegar into an ice tray and fill with water. After freezing, run the cubes though the garbage disposal, one at a time. This is an economical way to freshen this kitchen work-horse. Another method is to run 1/2 lemon through the disposal.

Freshen the inside of the microwave oven by washing it with a solution of baking soda. Dissolve 1 tablespoon in a cup of water, wipe with a clean cloth, and rinse in clear water.

Clean the inside of the refrigerator with baking soda. Make a solution of 1/2 cup of baking soda to a quart of warm water and wipe with a cloth wrung out in the solution. It will remove the food odors as well as clean and freshen the interior.

A sticking or dirty iron bottom can be cleaned by rubbing it on wax paper covered with a tablespoon of salt. Run the hot iron over the paper several times. Cool and wipe away the salt.

Coffee and tea stains can be removed from mugs and cups by scouring with baking soda sprinkled on a damp cloth. The baking soda will not scratch the surface, but should remove the stains.

Give new life to formica countertops—Make a solution of half vinegar and half water. Dip a cloth in this solution, wring it out and wipe the entire area. Finally, dry with a clean cloth. Extra hint: Keep a spray bottle of this mixture on hand for quick clean-ups on other kitchen surfaces such as appliances, table tops, light fixtures, and switches.

Cutting board odors—Wipe the board with a cloth or sponge sprinkled with baking soda. It will remove garlic, onion, fish, and most other food odors from wooden chopping boards.

Germs—When you bring groceries and drinks into your home from the super market, you have no idea where they have been or who may have handled them.

Wipe all lids before opening canned goods. Use a cloth which has been dipped in hot water and detergent and wrung out. If you drink directly from a bottle, wipe off the lip. Wipe off cartons before placing them in your refrigerator. You do not know where that cottage cheese, yogurt or milk carton has been before it came into your home.

Hand wash crystal glasses with 1/3 cup of vinegar added to detergent and warm water. The vinegar will help remove grease and mineral deposits and leave your fine crystal shiny bright.

Add sparkle to glasses and dishes—Pour 1/2 cup of vinegar into the automatic dishwasher during the last rinse cycle. Do not worry about the odor, it will be gone when the contents are dry.

When washing dishes by hand, add 1/2 cup of baking soda to your dishwater, along with your regular detergent. It will cut grease, remove fish odors and help soak off stubborn cooked-on food

Grease and odors on plastic dishes—Soak overnight in a solution of baking soda and water. Use four tablespoons to one quart of water. If the odor or grease is not gone, use baking soda sprinkled on a cloth or sponge, rinse and dry.

Black marks on floors can be removed without harm to the floor. Simply rub with a wet cloth sprinkled with dry baking soda and rinse with clear water.

To remove labels from bottles and jar, fill the container with water and place the lid on securely. Now it will stay submerged in the sink, allowing the label to dissolve quickly and evenly.

Clean light switch plates by placing them in the dishwasher. You may want to wait and do this when repainting. Place them on the top rack. Try only one plate first to be sure it is dishwasher safe.

Remove tarnish from pewter by rubbing it with a raw cabbage leaf.

Soak pots and pans in baking soda and water, while you are eating dinner. The baking soda will be working for you as you dine and clean-up will be much easier.

Rubber gloves will last longer if you buy them one size larger then you normally wear.

Rust on baking pans can be removed by scrubbing with a raw potato dipped in cleanser. Scouring with automatic dishwashing detergent will prevent scratching.

Prevent rust marks on cleaning containers that stain the surface under the sink. Place each can on a plastic lid. Save lids from containers such as powdered protein, yogurt, cottage cheese, popping corn, and other products.

Clean silver quickly. Place it in the sink, cover with warm water, two tablespoons of baking soda, and an aluminum lid.

Soak for a few minutes as you watch the tarnish disappear. Rinse in warm water and dry.

Prevent scouring pads from making a mess under the sink—Store them in plastic margarine containers or old soap dishes. Sea shells also make nice holders if the pads are stored on the counter top.

Water spots on stainless steel sinks—Wet a cloth with vinegar and apply to the sink. It will be sparkling clean. Use this method on any stainless steel pan or appliance. Do not worry about the odor, it will be gone when the surface is dry.

CHAPTER 2

In the Bathroom

Tub & Shower

On bathroom cleaning day clean the tub and shower as you finish your own personal cleaning. After your shower or bath, have your cleaning materials close at hand, so you can scrub the area before you get out. You will be so glad this job is done when you do the balance of the bathroom cleaning. Make certain the tub is non-skid if you stand in it without shoes.

Clean the bathtub with baking soda—Sprinkle a damp cloth with baking soda and gently scrub the surface. Rinse and shine with a dry cloth. It will clean and freshen the tub without the possibility of scratching. This method can also be used on bathroom fixtures. Remember, be careful while standing in the tub.

No bath soap will be wasted if you place the bar on a sponge. Scrub your body with this practical "soap dish" when you shower or bathe.

Mildew between bathtub tiles can be removed with rubbing alcohol or chlorine.

In-between caulking replacement, whiten the area with chlorine bleach. Pour a tablespoon of the chlorine into a small dish and apply with a cotton swab. Be sure the room is well ventilated. The chlorine can also be used on discolored tile grout.

Bathtub caulking will last longer if you wipe the shower tile, glass, and especially the caulking with a dry hand towel, after the last shower of the day. It only takes a few moments and will keep the caulking looking fresh and mildew-free longer. It will also cut down on soap scum. Perhaps the member of the family that takes the last shower can do the wiping. It might even encourage the children to take their showers first.

Soap scum on glass shower doors can be removed by scraping with a safety razor.

Soap scum and mildew on plastic sho
tains—Fill the tub with enough warm wate
the curtain, add ⅓ cup of your regular washing detergent and ½ cup of vinegar. Place the curtain in the
water. Swish it around so that the entire curtain is in
the water. Let it soak for ½ to one hour and check to see
if all the mildew is gone. If any remains, scrub gently
with a soft brush. Fill the tub with clear water to rinse.
Shake off excess water and rehang the curtain to dry,
with the bottom hem *in* the tub.

Clogged shower heads—Unscrew the head and
soak it in enough vinegar to cover. You may be able to
solve this problem without removing the head, by tying
a plastic bag securely around the head and carefully
filling it with vinegar. This will remove the minerals
that build up.

General

Pour hot, sudsy water into the toilet when you
finish cleaning. Not only will it help clean the toilet, but
it will reduce the water level so you can scour it properly without being hampered by the water.

Freshen the clothes hamper by placing a sheet of
fabric softener inside. It will freshen the bathroom and
the container. Either tape it or pin to the lid, depending
on the material of the hamper.

Plants in the bathroom—If you have a window,
this is a good spot for plants. Not only will it beautify
the room, but the plants will love the humidity caused
by showers and baths. Think about rotating plants to
this steamy atmosphere.

For a sweet smelling bathroom add a drop of
perfume to a light bulb. Be sure the light bulb is not

"on" and is cool. Use a delicate, fresh scent. When you turn on the light, it will radiate the fragrance as it becomes hot.

Prevent a steam-filled bathroom by starting the bath water with cold water only. Fill the tub with one or two inches of cold water and then add hot water to reach the desired temperature.

Brush your teeth with baking soda. It is non-abrasive to your teeth and you do not have to worry about fluoride, there is none in it. This natural substance is very economical to use. Keep a small covered container of it in the bathroom and pour about a teaspoonful into the palm of your clean hand. Wet your tooth brush and dab it in the baking soda. Brush in the usual manner. It will leave your teeth squeaky clean and your breath fresh too.

Always have a dry toothbrush ready for use. When shopping for new brushes, choose white or yellow ones for morning (representing the sun or light). For night time choose dark blue or black for a reminder of night. This will be an easy way to remember which brush to use.

Clean dentures by placing them in an ultra sound jewelry cleaner. Add enough water to cover and a small amount of mild detergent. Get an OK from your dentist before trying it.

Basin splashes can be removed by keeping a folded washcloth at the counter. The cloth can match the towels or the decor and will encourage family members to wipe up the counter area after each use at the basin.

Hair on floor, tub, or basin—Pick up with a dry cloth or tissue. The hair will cling more effectively than to a wet cloth, which seems to push the hair around, but does not pick it up.

Odors in drains—Pour ½ cup of vinegar into the drain. Do not use it for at least an hour, then run clear water to flush the vinegar away. If the odor returns, repeat.

Mildew on bathroom ceilings can be removed by rubbing with a damp cloth and chlorine bleach. The ceiling will look freshly painted. Be sure the room is well ventilated.

Welcome house guests with a basket of treats. On the counter in the bathroom that the visitor will use, fill a container with special soaps, lotion, after shave, tooth and nail brushes, deodorant, cologne, bath salts or anything that you know your guest likes. This is a great place to use samples and hotel soaps, lotions, shower caps, etc.

CHAPTER 3

In the Bedroom

Linens

Keep linens fresh on seldom used beds—Place a fabric softener sheet between the bed linen. The fabric softener will absorb any moisture and keep the linen sweet smelling. This is a good idea for your own bed if you are going to be away for an extended period.

Save wear and tear on sheets and reduce laundry loads—When changing the bed linen, remove only the bottom sheet and put the top sheet in its place. Add a clean top sheet. This method will only work if you use flat sheets.

During cold winters, use flannel sheets. It is so cozy to crawl into a bed that has warm sheets.

Make economical crib sheets and receiving blankets from one large flannel blanket. Cut the material to fit baby's crib and allow for a hem. Use leftover flannel for receiving blankets, bibs, and baby towels.

Sheets and pillow cases have so many uses around the house. When they are slightly worn or are no longer needed as linen, sheets and pillow cases can be used in other ways. Here are some suggestions:

1. Protect your mattress cover by placing a fitted sheet over it. This will reduce the laundering frequency and extend the life of the cover.
2. If you use a plywood "back" board protect your inner springs from the rough corners by placing a fitted sheet over the area.
3. Protect your inner springs from dust by attaching a fitted sheet to the underside.
4. Protect floors and carpets when repairs or painting are being done by placing a sheet in the area.
5. White sheets make good sun bathing blankets because they reflect more light. It is similar to lying

near water. Sheets are also less bulky to transport to your favorite sunning area. At the beach, sand shakes off the sheet easily.

6. In the garden, sheets can be used to hold weeds, leaves, and grass cuttings.
7. Protect lawn furniture by covering with sheets before winter storage.
8. Sheets can be made into pillow cases.
9. White sheets and pillow cases can be used for bandages. If you have checked the price of store-bought 4" x 4" gauze squares, you may think it worthwhile to try this: Cut the linen into 4" x 4" squares. Sterilize the squares by boiling for twenty minutes, when dry, store in a pillowcase that has been ironed.
10. Old white pillowcases can be used under regular cases to keep pillows clean longer.
11. A pillowcase makes a perfect bassinet sheet.
12. Make a Hallowe'en "ghost" decoration by using a white pillow case. Cut off the hem so the material will be more flimsy. With a black felt pen, draw a face on the upper half of the case. Make a small hole at the top so it can be hung from a hanger, and now you have a Hallowe'en mobile.
13. If you do not have a supply of sheets and pillowcases, look for them at garage sales and thrift shops.

General

Closets will smell fresh if you place a fabric softener sheet on the shelf.

Does the wind rattle a bedroom door? Does a door open and close loudly when you check a sleeping child or a person who is ill? Do you have a day sleeper?

Try this quick remedy: Tie one end of an old knit sock to the outside door knob and the other end to the inside knob. The door will close firmly, but more silently. If you like this idea you can make a more attractive door softener. Braid strips of cotton, wool, or nylon hose. Make it long enough to have a loop on each end to fit over the door knobs. To make the door even more quiet retract the latch by turning the knob, insert a straight pin into the latch between it and its plate and cover with a strip of plastic tape.

CHAPTER 4

In the Laundry Room

Ironing

Ironing board cover—After laundering, return it to the board before it is totally dry. The cover will fit more tightly as it dries. When it is completely dry, spray it with starch. This will keep it fresh and clean longer and the iron will glide over it more smoothly.

Embroidered pillow cases should always be ironed on the reverse side. This will make the stitches stand-out instead of flattening them as they would be when pressed on the right side.

Old hem lines can be removed by pressing the garment on the wrong side with a cloth soaked in vinegar. Use only on fabrics that can be laundered and only with as hot an iron as recommended for the specific material.

Pressing hair ribbons—Wash in a mild detergent and rinse. Roll in a paper towel (in case colors run) to remove excess water. Press on a paper bag that has been opened and flattened. Hold the ribbon firmly with one hand while you start ironing from the opposite end. Clean ribbons will only need dampening with water before pressing.

Large tablecloths will have fewer wrinkles if you fold them only enough to fit on a pants hanger. Hanging table covers, instead of folding them and placing them on a shelf, prevents many creases.

The Laundromat

At the laundromat—Leave those heavy boxes and bottles at home. Carry powdered detergent in a soiled, folded hand towel or in a soiled pillow case. Measure out enough for each load. Do the same with powdered bleach. Take liquid bleach in a small container with a tight fitting lid.

Correct change—Save quarters throughout the week. Give the store clerk even dollars so you can build your quarter bank.

Save time and energy when drying. After washing, separate all the delicate, synthetic and shrinkable clothing. Put those items that can be machine dried in the dryer for only two to three minutes. This will remove some of the wrinkles. Then, place them on hangers before returning home, where you can finish drying. Not only will you save money, but your clothes will last longer. (Follow this procedure at home as well).

Washing Machine

Soften and brighten clothes economically by adding 1 cup of vinegar to the last rinse water. The vinegar will remove all traces of soap scum or detergent.

Keep clothes white and bright—Never mix white clothes with colored clothes. Always separate the wash loads according to color.

Too much soap?—If your machine starts spewing out an abundance of suds, pour salt into the load. The foam will quickly disappear.

General

Remove lint from the dryer trap by scooping up most of it in your hand. Then use it to "sweep" the lint trap. The excess lint will cling and leave the trap lint-free.

Linens will last longer if you rotate them. When

putting away sheets, pillow cases, towels, and wash cloths always place them on the bottom of the stack so that everything will wear evenly.

Freshen and sterilize synthetic bed pillows between laundering.

Place them in the dryer on hot for a few minutes. This is especially helpful after someone in the family has been ill.

Shrunken woolens can sometimes be restored to their original shape by rinsing in soapy water instead of clear water. Soap softens wool.

Woolen sweaters will be softer if you add a tablespoon of vinegar to the final rinse water when washing by hand. Another method is to add one tablespoon of cream rinse to the last rinse water.

CHAPTER 5

General Cleaning

The secret to a clean *looking* home is to keep it picked up. Use it—put it away. Your abode will never look cluttered, or messy between cleanings if you practice this. The bonus is, you will always know where to find everything.

Carpets

Place door mats at all entrances to your home, both inside and outdoors. Do not forget the garage and patio. Shake, sweep and vacuum the mats often. They will protect your carpets and keep them clean longer.

Next time you have your carpets cleaned store some of those knick-knacks or delicate treasures in the kitchen. The oven, dishwasher, and refrigerator provide safe storage. To prevent an accident, tape a note to the oven and dishwasher dial as a reminder to remove the contents before using the appliance.

Cleaning a carpet without a vacuum cleaner— If your electric cleaner is on the fritz, or if you are without electricity, or at a rustic cabin, try this. Dampen paper towels and place across the length of one end of the carpet. Sweep the towels the entire length of the rug using a straw broom. The wet towels will keep the dust down and freshen the carpet. When finished, sweep the towels into a dust pan. They should be covered with lint and dust.

Shoes

After washing canvas tennis shoes, stuff each toe with a dry, thirsty washcloth. After the cloth has gobbled up most of the moisture, let the shoes air dry outdoors or near an open window. Be sure the laces are loosened and the tongue is raised to allow air to circulate more freely.

Canvas shoes can be cleaned quickly by spraying with carpet cleaning foam and then brushed. Repeat until all the soil is removed. This is a quick fix for washable tennis shoes when there is not enough time to wash and dry them in the machine. It may also extend the life of the shoe.

To freshen and absorb moisture sprinkle a small amount of baking soda into shoes. Keep a shaker filled with baking soda in the shoe closet for this purpose.

Protect dress shoes from heel smudges while driving. Use a pair of old or mis-matched men's socks. Cut off the toe and high top and use the remainder for a heel guard. Wear it over shoes while driving, but do not forget to remove it when you arrive at your destination!

Patent leather shoes can be cleaned with a damp cloth and hand soap. Petroleum jelly helps prevents cracking and makes the shoes look shiny. Rub a small amount into the leather and wipe with a soft tissue or rag.

Out of shoe polish?—Substitute paste floor wax. The neutral color will brighten light or dark leather shoes.

White shoe smudges or nicks can be repaired by using typewriter correction fluid before repolishing.

Stains

First let me tell you about Simple Green. In our house, we have a saying: "If it won't come clean, try Simple Green." We keep a diluted bottle of this biodegradable cleaner in the kitchen and another bottle in the car. It

removes spots from the carpet, from upholstered furniture, and from clothing (diluted). This super de-greaser
removes fish odors and grease from pans. We use it on
whitewall tires and car upholstery. On an outing Simple
Green removes insects and road grime from the grill,
headlights, and windshield (full strength). Cold water
acts as a catalyst, so Simple Green works well anyplace,
such as on a boat, at the cabin, and on camping trips. We
are always finding new uses for this super cleaner. Best of
all, it is economical to use and is now available at most
super markets and auto supply stores. If you can not locate Simple Green, write to the: Sunshine Makers, Inc.
Huntington Harbor, CA 92649. Be sure to follow the
manufacturer's directions.

BEFORE USING ANY OF THE FOLLOWING SUG-
GESTIONS FOR STAIN REMOVAL, FIRST TEST
THE SOLUTION ON A HIDDEN PART OF THE
FABRIC OR GARMENT.

Ballpoint pen marks on polyester fabrics can be
sprayed with hair spray. (But do not breathe the
fumes). The stain will usually disappear. If it does not
do the trick, and the material is washable, rub the area
with white tooth paste before washing.

Felt pen or oil pen marks on enamel walls can
be removed with brake fluid. Try it first on a small area
to make sure it is safe. Brake fluid is what some service
stations and restaurants use on graffiti.

Blood stains should be soaked in cold water immediately. Never put garments directly in the washer in
hot water, that will only set the stain. Hydrogen peroxide may also take out the stain.

Chewing gum stuck on clothing can be removed by holding a cube of ice directly on the area until the gum is hard. Scrape with a knife or pick off. Wash with warm soapy water.

Color crayon marks on wallpaper can be removed by rubbing gently with a damp cloth sprinkled with baking soda. Try it on an inconspicuous place first to test the paper.

Glue spills, (such as Elmer's Glue) can be wiped up with warm vinegar. Keep the vinegar handy while you are applying the glue for cleanup and washing your fingers.

Grass stains can be stubborn, but this usually works: soak the garment overnight in a gallon of cold water with ½ cup of ammonia. If this should fail, apply a solution of one part alcohol to two parts water. If the stain persists, use chlorine or peroxide bleach (use this method only on color-fast cotton fabric).

Grease on driveways and garage floors can be removed by following this procedure:

1. Cover grease spot with kitty litter, sawdust, or sand to absorb most of the moisture and sweep it up with an old broom.
2. Pour enough cola over the area to completely cover it.
3. Let it stand for at least 20 minutes, but make sure it does not dry.
4. Sweep it up with a broom. The grease spot should now be just a gray stain.
5. Bleach the stain with a solution of one cup detergent, one cup chlorine bleach, in one gallon of hot water. Let it soak for at least 15 minutes.
6. When the stain is gone, flush thoroughly with cold water.

Pencil marks can sometimes be removed with an eraser or by alternating applications of ammonia and detergent.

Pewter tarnish can be removed by rubbing the utensil with raw cabbage leaves.

Make your own pre-treat solution—

   1 cup of liquid dishwashing detergent
   1 cup ammonia
   1 cup of water

Place in a quart spray bottle and treat each garment as you throw it into the washer. This will remove blood (soak in cold water first) grass, and grease.

Red wine stains on washable fabrics can usually be removed by running them under cold water and then rubbing with a bar of soap. The soap changes the PH balance and turns the stain a light blue. This usually comes out when the fabric is laundered in the normal way. Salt is another method of removing wine stains. Sprinkle salt on the stain and rinse with cold water.

Rust can be removed from material by spreading the stained area over a pan of steaming water and then applying lemon juice directly to the stain. Rinse and repeat until the rust is completely gone.

Remove scorch marks on fabric by alternating applications of ammonia, detergent, and water. Rinse well before re-pressing. Another method that works well is to add a few drops of ammonia to one tablespoon of hydrogen peroxide. Rub the mixture into the fabric and rinse before ironing. Use this method on color-fast cotton fabrics only.

A shine on garments from ironing without a protective cloth, may be removed by the following: Make a solution of one tablespoon of vinegar in one cup of warm water. Rub into the fabric and rinse before re-pressing. Use this method on cotton or wool only.

Skunk scent can be removed from clothing by soaking it in tomato juice. Rinse thoroughly in cool water and launder in the normal manner.

Water rings on furniture are caused when liquid is trapped under the wax. Rings can sometimes be removed by rubbing the area with a mixture of half olive oil and half vinegar. Then, shine with a clean, dry cloth. Another method is to gently rub the ring with toothpaste and polish with a dry cloth. If the stain is stubborn, add a little baking soda to the toothpaste and repeat.

Miscellaneous

Freshen artificial flowers by placing them in a paper bag, with one cup of cornmeal. Close tightly and shake. Do this outdoors so you can remove the cornmeal from the flowers by shaking.

Computer and typewriter keys—Dust with a soft, clean paint brush. For thorough cleaning, wrap a damp cloth around the sharp end of a table knife or screw driver and carefully run between the rows of keys.

Piano keys—Wipe with a cloth slightly dampened with alcohol. Finish by wiping with a soft, dry cloth. Never use soap on the keys, it might yellow the ivory. Some marks may be removed with a soft eraser.

Save used fabric softener sheets for dusting— The sheets pick up dust, and will leave a fresh scent.

Clean the garage floor with water drained from the hot water tank. The tank should be drained annually to flush out sediment and minerals that collect there.

Lampshades and baskets can be dusted with a soft paint brush.

Remove soot from your fireplace chimney by

tossing two handfuls of table salt on a hot fire.

Protect fireplace tiles by washing them with warm sudsy water. After rinsing and drying, cover with a coat of floor wax.

Window cleaner—In an 8 ounce spray bottle, add three tablespoons of ammonia, one tablespoon of vinegar, and fill with water. Apply to only a small area at a time and polish with a soft, dry cloth before proceeding to the next section.

A House Cleaning Schedule

A House Cleaning Timetable is a general plan to help you stay on top of cleaning chores. The following is a basic schedule for cleaning your home. It is meant only as a guide. The chores can be adjusted, and added or subtracted to fit your own changing needs and the level of cleanliness you wish to obtain. Naturally, the size of your family and amount of traffic through your home will influence the frequency needed. If the jobs seem unsurmountable,stagger them so you never face too much to do at one time. The bonus is, you will never need to do "spring cleaning" again!

Kitchen

Weekly— Clean and disinfect all washable appliances, counter tops, cabinet fronts, furniture, and floors.

Monthly— Clean oven, stove-top burners and vent screen, refrigerator shelves, under sink, light fixtures, and windows. Wash silver and utensil drawers.

Annually— Clean vents, good China, silver, shelves and drawers, and change liners. Wash walls and ceiling, wash or dry clean curtains and shades.

Bathroom

Weekly—   Clean and disinfect shower, tub, faucets, glass doors, counter tops, cabinet fronts, basins, mirrors, soap dishes, light fixtures, floors, toilet, and wall near toilet. Replace towels and clean brushes and combs.

Monthly—   Wipe shelves and drawers, straighten and clean linen closet, and medicine cabinet. Clean shower door tracts, wash windows, light fixtures, and shower curtain.

Annually— Replace caulking, clean vent, wash walls, ceiling, and wash or dry clean curtains.

Bedrooms

Weekly—   Change linen, dust furniture, lamps, pictures, books, and bric-a-brac. Vacuum carpets, and/or clean floors, and light switches.

Monthly—   Wash windows, clean baseboards, vacuum closets, wash mirrors, dust clothing storage bags, and polish furniture. Launder mattress pad.

Annually— Launder dust ruffle, turn mattress and box spring, wash or dry clean spread, comforter, blankets, and pillows. Clean out and sort contents of closets and drawers.

Living/Dining/Family Rooms

Weekly—   Dust furniture, pictures, books, and lamps. Vacuum carpets or clean floors. Polish mirrors, and TV and computer screens. Clean and disinfect telephones.

Monthly—   Clean baseboards and area between wall
and carpet. Clean woodwork and vacuum
upholstery. Clean computer, typewriter,
and piano keys. Wash light fixtures, vases,
figurines, picture glass, and any other
washable objects.

Annually—   Professionally clean carpets and upholstery. Remove lampshades and take outdoors to brush. If washable, clean with
detergent and water.

Porches and Patios

Weekly—   Sweep, clean with detergent and hot
water, and hose off. Clean doors, knobs,
and thresholds. Clean entry floors. Shake,
sweep, or vacuum mats.

Miscellaneous

Weekly—   Dust curtain rods, tops of drapes, levelor
slats, artificial flowers and books. Sweep
and hose off walkways. Clean and disinfect door knobs and handles.

Monthly—   Clean sliding door tracts, casings and
doors. Clean and disinfect waste paper
baskets and indoor garbage cans. Wash or
hose door mats and throw rugs.

Annually—   Remove and clean door and window
screens. Remove and clean levelor slats
and pull cords. Clean, sort, and straighten
storage areas and garage. Scrub outdoor
garbage cans.

CHAPTER 6

Green Things

ıts

House plants may be more than decorative— Scientists are finding that common house plants such as daisies, mums, lilies, and philodendron, may actually be absorbing the indoor pollutants caused by organic chemicals that are emitted from synthetic compounds found in building materials and furniture. New homes and office buildings are now built more airtight and hold many gasses in a concentrated area.

When repotting house plants with soil that has been used outdoors, bake the soil in the oven for at least twenty minutes to keep plants parasite-free. Before placing the dirt in the oven, make sure it is quite dry. Place it in a flat container, such as a cookie sheet and cover with foil. This will prevent any parasites from escaping into the oven. The oven should be pre-heated to 400 degrees F. You can also use the microwave oven for sterilizing the soil. Set the oven for five minutes on high. Use a glass or plastic container and cover loosely.

A good place to shop for greenery is a company that rents plants to offices. Some of these businesses recycle plants they can no longer rent. You can "adopt" a plant at a fraction of its retail cost. 8" or 10" potted plants such as Boston ferns or palms go for as little as $1 to $3. Look in the telephone book to find a plant leasing company in your area, and start asking questions.

African violets are delicate plants that should be watered from the bottom with tepid water to prevent spotted leaves. If you must water from the top, pour water directly on the root area, without letting the water touch the leaves. You may also find that African violets will bloom once again. These plants like to be pot-bound, so when you re-pot, they may not bloom until the following year.

Basil—This easy-to-grow herb will flourish with lots of sun and frequent fertilizing. This common herb is the main ingredient in pizza and pasta sauce, and will give recipes a special fresh taste.

Boston ferns are not gypsies, they will flourish if you keep them in one spot they can call home.

Bougainvillea will bloom *more* if you water and fertilize *less*.

Bulbs should not have their leaves cut off until they turn yellowish brown. Before that, they are still feeding the bulb and preparing it for next year's blooms.

Chrysanthemums—After growing to five or six inches tall, the plant should be pinched down about one inch. Do this in May, June, or July. This will create sturdy, fuller plants with more flowers.

Color all summer—These flowers will insure blooms continually throughout the season:

- Perennials: Geranium, blue salvia, gloriosa, daisy, and rose.
- Annuals: Cosmo, impatiens, petunia, allysum, and marigolds.

Dahlia bulbs will have larger, more beautiful blooms if you soak them in water overnight before planting.

Perennials—When planting your garden make a definite plan first. Perennials last a long time. Make sure you get what you want. Plan carefully to have more color during the year. Remember to ask how large a bush will grow and note how close to a window, wall, or walk it is being planted. Roots can do much damage over time if they are too near pipes, walks, or walls. If you have an annual outdoor party, such as on The Fourth of July, you may want to plan to have as many things as possible blooming at once to add to the festivity.

A friend of mine has eight flowering plum trees in her front yard. They are in full bloom each year on her daughter's birthday (February 22). What a magnificent present!

Petunias will bloom profusely if you pluck off the old blooms as they die. Be sure to get the hip part of the bloom (the part that holds the stem of the flower). This old blossom is still sapping energy from the plant as long as it is in place.

Poinsettias will bloom again the following year if you do this: At the end of October, put the plant in a very dark closet for thirteen hours of darkness and then move it to a bright room for eleven hours. This must be done daily until it blooms. By Christmas, it should be in its full splendor. October or November is also the best time to transplant last year's poinsettia.

Roses will bloom again sooner if you cut the flower stem just above a five leaflet-leaf. Do this for cut flowers and when getting rid of wilted flowers.

Roses that are not so "rosy"—If your roses are sickly, you can be the doctor by knowing what is literally eating them.

- Rose slugs make small holes in the leaves.
- Spider mites make tiny yellow spots when they feed on the underside of the leaf.
- Aphids suck on the buds and tips of the stems and actually drain the life out of the plant and deform the buds.

Spray plants with detergent and water before they have a problem. Do this on a regular basis as a preventative. If you already have a problem ask your nursery expert for the proper spray.

Snip shoots that often appear at the base of a plant. The shoots sap energy.

For a late summer splash of color, select marigolds, zinnias, lobelia and petunias.

Shasta daisies will have larger flowers if you separate the clumps every two years.

Short on garden space?—Plant vegetables in containers on your sunny patio or porch. Carrots, lettuce, beets, and chard all have interesting leaves. They can also be mixed with flowers.

Plant marigolds and cosmos near vegetables as a natural bug deterrent. The insects do not like the odor.

Move seedlings easily with less chance of transplant shock. Line strawberry baskets with a thin layer of newspaper. Fill with dirt and plant the seeds. When the plant is ready to transplant, lift the seedling, newspaper and all, into its new home in the ground.

Seedling labels can be made from empty Clorox bottles. After thoroughly rinsing, cut out pieces of the plastic 1" by 3" or 4". Make one end of the label pointed to stand in the soil. Label it with a marking pen.

Cut Flowers

Keep cut flowers smelling sweet—Place a piece of charcoal in the vase water. A sprig of mint will also keep the water fresh and add a clean smelling fragrance to your arrangement.

Look for flower containers at flea markets and garage sales. You may find unique pitchers, bowls, perfume bottles, jars, or anything that will show off a bouquet. If you visit a sick friend in the hospital or at home, you can surprise the patient with a garden bouquet in a lovely, but inexpensive container. You can also use these vessels for other gift giving. Add a pretty bow for a finishing touch.

Make a custom fitting frog for flower arrangements. Criss-cross strips of plastic tape over the top of a vase and arrange the flowers between the strips.

Clean a dirty vase by filling it with vinegar and soaking it for at least one half hour. Wash with a cloth in warm soapy water and rinse. All mineral deposits and flower decay will be gone. If the vase has a narrow neck, add some pop corn kernels and shake, or use a bottle brush.

Fertilizing

Chimney soot makes a fine fertilizer for the garden and potted plants. Mix it into the soil.

Fireplace ashes—Carefully spread around the garden and mulch into the soil.

Soak egg shells in water—Pour the water on garden plants and mulch the broken shells into the soil.

Spraying

1. Read the manufacturer's instructions before beginning. You may damage more than the plant. The spray could be dangerous to your health if used improperly.
2. Spray in the cool morning or evening, never during the heat of the day.
3. Never spray when the soil is dry. Moist plants handle spray better.
4. Spray the *under* side of the leaf to completely destroy pests. If you only spray the tops, the bugs will hide underneath and continue their meal with hardly a pause.

5. Discourage flies and aphids. Spray plants with detergent added to water (one teaspoon of detergent to a pint of water). Do not spray when flowers are blooming, it may damage the petals. Instead, wipe each leaf with a cloth that has been wrung out in the detergent solution.

Watering

Roots will go deeper if you water thoroughly. They will also need less water.

The following plants have beautiful flowers, but do not require much water once they have reached maturity.

- Annuals: blue salvia, allysum, vinca rosea and portulaca.
- Perennials & Ground Covers: coreopsis, ice plant, geraniums, pelargoniums, and rosemary.

Reduce watering by 30 to 50%—Polymers can help save water. They are granules that store water. When placed in the soil, polymers save water and release it to the roots as needed. It works on indoor or outdoor plants. These little "camels of the soil" help solve the problem of frequent watering when you are away. Look for them at your gardening supply store.

A Wall Garden—If you are short of space, or just for the added beauty, attach boxes filled with flowering plants to a wall or fence. Not only will this wall garden save space, it will allow patio or yard cleaning without moving containers. Plants should be chosen according to how much direct sun the area gets. Watch the wall throughout the day and note what exposure it receives before deciding what to plant.

Water roses well when the temperature soars, but do it in the morning, never in the heat of the day.

Check hanging baskets daily in summer for dryness. The combination of high temperatures and wind dry out soil quickly.

Save water from boiled eggs for watering. This liquid contains minerals and makes a beneficial drink for house and garden plants.

A worn out garden hose can start a new life as a soaker. Use your ice pick to make uniform holes.

Miscellaneous

Turn clay pots into decorator items—Cover the pots with remnants of material to match the decor of a room. Use pinking shears to cut strips of material about two and one half inches wide and five inches long. Glue them to an eight inch pot, overlapping the strips until the surface is covered. Also cover the inside of the pot, about two inches below the rim, or below the soil level. Do not cover the hole in the bottom of the container. Coat with clear shellac. Add a plant and you have a nice gift, for yourself or a friend.

Drain dishes for house plants—Look for dinner or salad plates at garage sales, flea markets, or department and dime store sales. If you are patient, you can find pretty dishes to catch the excess water when you over-water.

When working or playing in the yard place a clock in the window. You can check the time without tracking in. This is great for the children.

Protect hands while pruning roses or thorny bushes. Wear old, heavy potholder mitts.

CHAPTER 7

Repairs & Decorating

General

Re-string broken beads with dental floss. It will be stronger than the original string.

Cracks in china can sometimes be repaired by simmering in milk for 40 minutes. The black line should disappear and the piece of china will be stronger.

Contact lens lost in drains. This can happen to anyone. First be sure to close the drain when inserting or removing lens. Invest in a large wrench. If you should lose a lens do not run water. Shut off the water and place a bucket under the sink. Remove the U-shaped sink trap by loosening the slip nuts with your new wrench. Pour the excess runoff water into the pail and look for your contact lens. If it is not in the pail, pour water through the sink trap as the lens may be stuck to the inside. Have a glass of water ready to flush the trap.

Prevent plywood from splitting—Place masking tape where you intend to saw.

Extend the life of sandpaper—Before using, moisten the reverse side of this abrasive with water. You will also find it more pliable and easier to use.

Small holes in screens—Wipe or brush any transparent glue into the holes.

Screws may be inserted more easily if they are first rubbed on a piece of soap or candle wax.

Doors

Doors that stick—Place a sheet of carbon paper (carbon side up) in the problem area on the frame. Close and open the door a few times, then file or sand where you see a carbon mark. This is similar to the way a dentist finds a "high" spot on your tooth.

Squeaky door hinges—Spray with Pam. No mess and it will penetrate inside the hinge. Vegetable oil can also be rubbed or sprayed on the hinge. Be sure to protect the floor before starting.

Drawers

Sticking drawers can be eased by applying soap or wax to the runners, guides, and other sticking spots. Sometimes steel thumbtacks can be inserted into the front of the runner or the back of the drawer where the two make contact. This prevents wood-to-wood wear and provides a smoother surface on which the drawer can slide.

Restore wooden drawers—Sand the inside surface using an electric sander or do it by hand. If you move to an older home or one that has been neglected, the sanding will remove dirt, grime, and roughness. You can remove years of grubby soil from silverware drawers or chest of drawers. After sanding is completed, you can decide whether to refinish or enjoy the new surface.

Knobs on cupboards and drawers will stay tighter longer if you apply clear nail polish or glue to the screw, before inserting.

Painting

Before painting cabinets and doors, cover all hardware with petroleum jelly, it will aid in wiping up drips. Use petroleum jelly on hands before starting. Be sure to lubricate around fingernails and cuticles. This will make clean-up easier.

Cabinet handles are very expensive. It will cost over $100 to replace the handles for an average kitchen and bathroom. Wooden or metal hardware can look like new by repainting. Remove the handles and wash them in a mild detergent. Prepare them for painting by mounting them on heavy cardboard. Cut pieces of cardboard carton lids into sizes big enough to hold ten or twelve handles. Poke holes with an ice pick to fit the screws of each handle. After placing the screws in place, attach a handle to each screw. Now you are ready to spray paint in the same or contrasting color that will be used on the cabinets. The cardboard will allow you to get good paint coverage. You may want to give the handles two or three coats because of the constant use they receive. The handles will have a completely new and fresh look and save money too.

Protect shoes while painting—Wear old socks or place plastic bags over shoes. Make sure they fit snugly to prevent tripping. Secure the bags with rubber bands or cover them with the feet of old panty hose.

For spills and splatters of water base paint, keep a damp cloth nearby for quick wipe ups. If you wipe the drips immediately before the paint sets, they will come off cleaner and with less muscle.

Paint cabinets, bookcases, and moldings with heavy duty, outdoor, water-base, enamel paint. This product is more durable and will last longer for items that are in constant use.

Pausing before the job is finished—Brushes used in water-base paint can be stored in a jar of water while you stop for short periods (1–2 hours). When you return, take the brush outside and shake out the water over a newspaper or into a trash can. Indoors, you can place the brush in a plastic bag and squeeze the water out.

A less messy method when you stop is to place the

paint brush in a ziplock plastic bag and seal it. For oil base-paint, put the package in the freezer, the oil will prevent freezing. For water-base paint, place the package in the refrigerator. Either way, when you resume painting, the brush will be ready. You can use plastic wrap in place of the bag, just make sure you seal the brush properly so that no air can penetrate.

Remove water-base paint from hands and face with shaving cream or shampoo.

Old, neglected paint brushes may come clean if you soak them in hot vinegar.

Leftover paint—If you have a pint or less, transfer it to a glass jar with a tight-fitting lid. The paint will come in handy for touching up nicks and gouges, and the paint job will last longer. Label the *lid* (it has less chance of getting splattered with paint) with the date, the areas painted, color, brand, stock number, and the store where purchased. This information will help if you paint with the same color next time, or if you liked the paint enough to purchase it again.

Scissors

Dull scissors can be sharpened by cutting a piece of fine sandpaper with one or two snips.

When scissors bind or grab, rub them with your fingers. The natural oil in your skin will provide needed lubrication without the danger of damaging fabric or paper.

Scratches

Light scratches on wood can be removed by

rubbing with the cut surface of walnut or brazil nut meat.

Scratches on panelling, floors, or doors can be hidden with dyed wax, available at hardware stores.

Walls

Find wall studs by passing a compass over the wall. When the compass needle wavers, it has located the nails in the stud. Once you find one stud, the rest are usually 16 inches apart.

Prevent plaster from cracking when hanging pictures. Place a piece of transparent tape over the area where the nail hanger will enter the wall.

Pictures will hang straighter if you use two hangers side-by-side, instead of one.

Prevent wall marks made by furniture that is placed too close to the wall. Rubber bumpers, the type used on toilet seat lids, can be attached to the back of bookcases, desks or any piece of furniture that comes in contact with the wall. Use two or three bumpers, depending on the size of the furniture. It will protect the piece as well as the wall. Ask for these protective bumpers at any hardware or plumbing supply house. Good for kid's rooms.

Patch plaster on walls by mixing spackling compound with the same color paint originally used.

Fill nail holes in white walls with white tooth paste for a temporary fix until the area is repainted.

Decorating

Rooms will look larger if you paint the base boards the same color as the floor covering.

Give a room that decorator touch by adding a few oversized items, such as: Large cushions, plants, baskets, lamps, statues, vases, or pictures.

Frame special greeting cards as a wall grouping that you can enjoy every day.

Wallpaper makes attractive and durable shelf and drawer liners. Pick a pattern from remnants or discontinued stock. Many wall coverings are more economical then shelf paper.

CHAPTER 8

Saving Water & Energy

We often take the basics, like water and heat, for granted. All we have to do is turn on a faucet or push a button and we are clean and comfortably warm. We do not always think how much of our precious resources we are using until there is a drought or a utility rate hike. Following are some ways to cut down on your utility bills and help your community at the same time.

Bathing—Try these suggestions to save water, electricity and time:

1. A shower flow restrictor can save a family of four an average of 1,600 gallons of water each month and you probably will not even notice the difference. Remember, you are not only paying for the water, but for heating it as well. Ask your utility company for a shower flow restrictor. It comes with simple installation instructions.

2. A five minute shower may use 30 gallons of water. Time your shower so you do not exceed the five minute mark. Some utility companies offer a timer to place in the shower. The cost is about $5.00.

3. An even more effective way to save is to turn on the shower only long enough to get wet. Turn it off while you lather up and scrub, then turn on the water for a fast rinse. This method uses only about four gallons of water.

4. When you first turn the shower on, the water is cold and is usually wasted. Collect this water in a bucket for watering plants.

5. Consider taking a bath instead of a shower. A partially filled tub uses less water than the average shower.

6. Bathe small children together. It is fun for them and saves time as well as energy and is something you can do together.

Ceiling fans can reduce heat consumption drastically. In winter, a fan can circulate heat more efficiently and keep it off of ceilings. In summer, the fan helps to keep you cool by drying the perspiration on your skin. This enables you to be more comfortable at higher temperatures and reduce the use of air conditioning. A good ceiling fan will use very little energy.

Automatic dishwasher—Wait until the dishwasher is full before operating. This will save water and electricity. Shut it off when the drying cycle begins (set an alarm or use the stove timer). Prop the door open slightly with a dish cloth or utensil and let the contents air dry. This will save 75% of the electricity used for the load.

Dishwashing by hand—Do not run water continuously. Use one sink or pan full of rinse water.

Garbage disposal—Use cold water, not hot, to flush. The hot water may cause problems with melting grease which later congeals in the pipes.

Drinking water—Keep a container of water in the refrigerator instead of running the tap water until it is cold each time you want a drink.

Turn dual faucets to the "COLD" setting. As the faucet is turned on it will not draw from the hot water tank each time. When you use "HOT" water, get in the habit of turning the faucet back to the "COLD" position as you finish.

Keep drapes and shades closed on winter evenings. This will help reduce heat loss through the glass.

Preparing vegetables and fruits—Use a pan or sink full of water for cleaning. Do not let the water run during this operation.

Hot water tank—Wrap a blanket around the tank. Bind it with rope. This will prevent heat loss and save electricity. Caution—If you have a gas hot water tank heater, keep the blanket away from the small burner door.

Oven—Turn off the oven before the last few minutes of baking time. The oven will retain enough heat to finish baking and also save energy. After baking in the winter, open the oven door to warm the room with the heat left inside.

Bake in the evening—In winter, it will help heat the house. In summer, it will keep the house cooler during the heat of the day.

Use less energy and keep the kitchen cool in summer. Bake in the microwave oven or toaster oven for small quantities. These small appliances use less energy than a full sized oven.

Toilet leaks—Place four drops of blue or green food coloring in the tank. Then watch for any color that seeps into the toilet (do not flush it). Wait about fifteen minutes and check for color in the bowl. If you find any, the plunger ball may need replacing. Do not worry about the color, it will dissipate after a few flushings (if you use only food coloring). If water is flowing above the overflow pipe, the water level is too high. This can be adjusted by carefully bending the float arm down so the valve shuts off sooner. The ballcock may need replacing if the water is running continuously. Toilets are noted for leaks, so yours may be suspect if you are receiving higher water bills.

Toilet Flushing—Each time a toilet is flushed it uses between five and seven gallons of water. Reduce this amount by the following methods:

1. Place a plastic bag or plastic bottle, filled with water into the tank. Be sure to soak off any label on the bottle. The bottle will displace some of the water. The toilet will still work efficiently if you

make sure the bottle or bag does not interfere with the flushing mechanism. Do not use a brick as it could crack the toilet tank.

2. Do not flush every time the toilet is used.
3. Do not use the toilet as a garbage can. Do not put Q tips, wrappers, cigarettes or any other refuse into the toilet.
4. When looking for a new toilet, shop for one of the energy-saving models. They have a shallow trap and use only about 3-1/2 gallons of water per flush. Commercial models can be adapted for use in your home. They have a pressure feature that uses air to assist with the flushing.

Washing machine—Save soiled laundry until you have a full load, unless you have a water level control on your machine. Use a detergent that works well in cold water. You will have an added bonus, your clothes will last longer and stay brighter.

CHAPTER 9

Pest Control

Ants can be discouraged with vinegar. After you locate where they are entering your home, wipe the area with vinegar, repeat until they are gone.

Discourage stray cats from using your flower beds and boxes for waste elimination. Insert wooden or plastic chopsticks into the soil. Place them about eight to ten inches apart. This will make it difficult for the feline to squat. Adding manure to the soil will help your plants grow, also deter the animal. Cats like clean dirt. The fertilizer will trick them into thinking another cat has been there first. Cayenne pepper mixed in the soil is another deterrent.

Discourage wild deer from eating garden plants and flowers. Mix hair into the soil. The odor from human hair will keep these lovely, but pesky creatures away plants. Ask for cuttings at your local beauty or barber shop.

Vacuum cleaners are prolific breeding grounds for fleas—Cut a two inch strip from the end of a new flea collar and place it in the vacuum bag. Replace it often if the bag is the permanent type. If you use a disposable bag, add the strip to each bag replacement.

Insect bites—Make a paste of baking soda and apply to the area. This will relieve pain and swelling. If not available, temporarily use mud. Vitamin E will relieve the itching. Break open a capsule and apply.

Mice and squirrels will vacate your attic if you put out mothballs.

Moths and silverfish—Keep your closets and drawers free of these insects by placing cedar chips in the areas. Fill cloth bags with the wood particles and place them in drawers, on closet shelves. or tied to hooks or clothes hangers. Cedar has a fresh pungent odor.

Skunks can be a nuisance around rural homes. First, find where they have made their new headquar-

ters. They like to be under a pile of boards, in a basement corner, or attic. Soak a cloth with household sudsy
ammonia and leave it where you have seen traces of
this "striped kittycat."

Next time you spray the interior of your home
for insects remember the oven, dishwasher, and refrigerator are air-tight. Use these appliances to store foods
during the spraying operation.

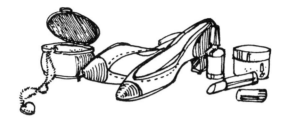

CHAPTER 10

Just for You

Clothing & Accessories

Accessories can be kept in clear plastic, hanging shoe racks. Group them according to color and what you wear together. For example, in one compartment store red earrings, bracelet, matching scarf, shoe bows, gloves, stockings, lapel pin, or anything else you may choose to wear together. When dressing to go out, it will no longer be necessary to hunt for each item.

Check the lingerie department when looking for ladies eveningwear. You may find a treasury of unique, feminine frocks at a fraction of the cost of evening dresses and pants. Use your imagination to get as slinky as you care to.

Ladies, consider wearing mens' shirts with suits, skirts, and pants. Shirts of fine quality can be found at better prices than women's blouses. Look for them on sale. Now that men are no longer limited to basic colors, you will have a wide variety from which to choose. Add a lacy tie or pearls for a feminine accent. No one will know you are wearing a man's shirt, unless you wish to tell them. The only difference is the price; and men's shirts button the opposite way.

Tall or larger women—For clothes that really fit, try looking in the men's department when you are shopping for sweat clothes, pants, tops, and socks.

Tiny women can shop in the children's department of better ready-to-wear stores. The prices are much less, the clothes are chic, but most of all, they fit!

Do you misplace your wallet? This can be disastrous if you are away from home! Just to be safe, pin your wallet to the inside of your purse with strong ribbon that is at least a foot long. This will allow you full use of your wallet when you take it out, but will not let you leave it behind.

Panty Hose

Wear gloves while donning panty hose—This will prevent snags made from fingernails or rough hands.

Wearing panty hose can be a winter comfort—They are especially beneficial to keep out the cold when practicing winter sports such as skiing, skating, or sledding.

Save panty hose with runs and snags to wear under pants.

Panty hose will last longer if you buy light support. Besides wearing longer, they look good and the support is beneficial to your legs, especially if you are on your feet much of the time.

Save the support tops of pantyhose—When the legs are no longer wearable, cut them off and use the tops under shorts, or for any occasion when you do not want to wear hose.

Turn support panty hose tops into strapless sun bras—They can be worn at home while gardening, sunning, or under low cut summer dresses.

Shoes

Prevent slipping with new shoes—Sandpaper the soles. This is a good safeguard for children's new shoes also.

Squeaky shoes can be silenced by piercing the soles with several small holes, this will relieve the pressure. The holes should be placed right behind where the ball of the foot rests.

Personal

For an unbelievable pick-me-up, try this—Fill

the tub with warm water and one cup of 3% hydrogen peroxide. Lie in the tub, submerged to the neck, for at least 20 minutes. You will feel very light, and invigorated, and ready to tackle the world. This is especially helpful if you must attend an evening meeting after a tiring day.

Egg white facial—Wash your face thoroughly and apply egg white liberally to your face and neck. Leave it on for 15 to 30 minutes. Your face will feel very tight as the liquid dries. Rinse with cool water and dry with a soft towel. This treatment will help clean deeply, your pores will look smaller, and your face will be shiny clean. The egg white facial can be used without wasting the remainder of the egg. Make a small hole in the end of the egg with a pin and carefully crack it around the hole. Make the opening about ¼ inch in diameter. Shake out as much egg white as needed and place transparent tape over the hole. Return the egg to the carton, with the covered hole upright.

Hair on arms and legs can be bleached easily by using two parts bleaching peroxide (20% by volume) and one part ammonia. Add a small amount of detergent or lotion to give the solution substance and mix in a plastic bottle. Before applying, test a small amount on your arm and wait fifteen minutes to be sure your skin is not sensitive to the mixture, and then proceed. Apply to the areas to be bleached and leave on until you see it working. It may bleach the hair in as little as fifteen minutes, or it may take up to an hour. If you apply the solution in the sun it will work much faster. Rinse thoroughly when you are finished and apply a moisturizing lotion. This treatment may last for several weeks, depending on how fast your hair grows and how dark it is. In summer, it will last longer if you spend time in the sun.

Home treatment for dry or damaged hair—Rub Best Foods Mayonnaise into your hair. Wrap your head in plastic wrap. Wear it all day, or for at least six hours. The plastic will keep the warmth of your body heat working on the oil and egg in the mayonnaise. Shampoo your hair at least twice and rinse thoroughly in clear water. Your hair will be soft, shiny, and very manageable. Use this treatment as often as you please. A good time to do this is when you are house cleaning and do not have any social or business plans.

A natural laxative—Drink a glass of water the first thing in the morning. The water may be cool or warm, whichever you prefer, but drink it the first 3 to 5 minutes after you arise. It stimulates the intestines and usually works within a few minutes. If you do not like the taste of plain water, add a squeeze of fresh lemon.

Get more mileage from lotions—As a bottle becomes empty, prop it in a corner, upside down. Most of the liquid will be near the opening instead of wasted at the bottom. To get even more of the lotion from plastic bottles, cut off the bottom. To do this, place the bottle on a bread board and carefully cut it open with a knife. Keep the container in a plastic bag to prevent drying. Using every drop is especially worth the effort with expensive sun screens.

Dry skin softener—Add one cup of milk to your bath water for soft, smooth skin. The protein in the milk does the job by moisturizing your skin. It will not leave the tub slippery as some bath oils do.

Soften hands while you sleep. In the evening, perhaps while watching TV, massage heavy duty lotion or petroleum jelly into your hands. Lotions containing glycerin are usually very effective. Leave the lubricant on your hands and wear cotton gloves to bed.

Soften and refresh feet while you sleep—Do the same as above and wear socks to bed. Witch hazel makes a relieving wash for tired or aching feet. Simply wipe your "tootsies" with cotton splashed with this alcoholic, but not drying, solution. Witch hazel is distilled from the bark of the tree.

Sunburn—Sprinkle ¼ cup of baking soda into a tub of water and soak for 20 minutes for a cooling, relieving effect. Another very effective way to relieve sunburn pain is to pat it with a cloth soaked in vinegar. At first, it may sting, but it will reduce the pain and burning within minutes.

If sunscreen makes your face break out, try changing brands until you find the right one for you. Wear a good moisturizer beneath it. Clinique has a sports makeup that provides some sun protection. It contains a small amount of sunscreen and does not seem to cause any problem to skin.

Sweet Dreams

Would you like to remember what you dream?—When you are cozy and relaxed, ready to visit The Land of Nod, program yourself by saying "I am going to remember what I dream tonight." In the morning, as you waken, think what thoughts are going through your mind. Keep a paper and pencil by your bed so you can jot down these first thoughts. At least one of your nightly dreams will become quite clear. This will be helpful to the skeptic who does not believe he dreams. If you want to learn more about your dreams, get a dream interpretation book. After you make your daily notes, look them up in your new book. You may be surprised at this insight into your personality.

Sleep more soundly—To unwind before retiring, try any of the following: 1) Brush your hair. 2) Remove make-up and massage your face with cream. 3) Massage your feet. Massage the pads of your toes with the eraser of a pencil. Then rub in lotion. 4) Relax in a bubble bath. 5) Drink warm milk. 6) Read something light. 7) Listen to relaxing music. DO NOT eat, watch the news, or an exciting TV program.

Meeting New Friends

Meet dynamic people and improve yourself at the same time. Consider attending a Toastmasters' meeting. There is no obligation or pressure to join and you cannot help but be impressed by these positive, enthusiastic, and dynamic speakers. In no time at all you will be able to speak in front of a group, just like a pro. After only a few meetings, you will see a definite improvement in yourself—more confident, articulate, organized, and happier. It could change your life.

Meeting compatible, new people is easy if you just do what *you* like to do. Take a class. Some sport, such as golf, swimming, tennis, skiing, or sailing will bring people into your sphere that like the same things that you like. Perhaps a craft class such as art, pottery making, or a music class is something that interests you. Do not forget volunteer work for meeting new friends and doing something for the community as well. Any of the above suggestions are also ways to meet people when you have moved to a new area. It puts you on the "inside of the circle."

Miscellaneous

A book mark that will always be there when you need it. Place a rubber band between the pages. Make sure it is loose enough so that the pages will not be damaged. Each time you stop reading, move it to your new place.

Unravel that tangled gold chain by gently rubbing it between your hands. Just like magic, it will straighten out.

Help prevent lipsticks from breaking—Never screw the cylinder up any further than necessary. The lip rouge usually breaks because it is top-heavy. If it should break, try putting it back in place by applying some pressure, and store it in the refrigerator for a couple of hours. It may mend.

Make nail polish last longer—Before applying nail polish, clean your nails with vinegar. The polish will go on easier and last longer. It is like putting paint on a clean wall.

Over 55?—Always ask for a senior discount wherever you shop, dine, or travel.

CHAPTER 11

Just for Kids

Big Kids

Be Your Own Boss This Summer

Another summer will be here before you know it. Did you ever dream of having your own business? Being the boss, making decisions, and even making money?

Yes, you too can be an entrepreneur. Simply start in your own neighborhood. In most communities there are many people who need services you can provide. Some adults who work at a job do not have time to do many necessary home tasks. Others cannot, or may not want to shop, wash windows, clean, repair, cook, or garden. Shut-ins do not always have someone available to do chores, write letters, or exercise and bathe their pets. Seniors sometimes need assistance getting to and from medical appointments, visiting friends, attending church, or going to the beauty or barber shop. They may also need help with home tasks. Women living alone sometimes need help with simple repairs or installation of small appliances, but cannot afford the cost of a carpenter or electrician. Moving a large picture to a new location or hanging a curtain may be more than some people can manage.

You can start earning money performing many services while making a worthwhile contribution to your community. Not a bad feeling!

Planning—First, make a list of all the services you could provide. Here are some examples:

Vacation house sitting	Ironing clothes
Vacation telephone service	Yard maintenance
Vacation plant & yard care	Rearranging furniture
Household & office moving	Shampooing carpets
Exercising animals	Going on vacation to share
Detailing cars	child care

Shopping

Sewing/mending

Accompanying a child or
adult to an appointment

Preparing meals

Assisting w/party
preparation

Providing party music or
entertainment

Providing a party DJ

Caring for party guests'
children

Shampooing, setting, or
cutting hair

House painting

Holiday or store window
painting & decorating

Do any, or none of the above, but think of things you would be good at doing and perhaps even enjoy. Work should be fun whenever possible!

Do you have a special talent you can put to use? Can you offer tutoring to a child who has been ill or could not keep up with daily school work? Can you help a poor reader, improve someone's French, or backstroke? Perhaps you can hold a summer class or private tutoring in auto repair, pottery making, repairing or clothes makeover, sailing, swimming, exercise, or any craft or sport. All those computers that are still sitting in a dark closet only need a catalyst to get their poor, intimidated, owners "on line."

Getting started—Let people know about your services. Do not hide your "light under a bushel basket." A handbill is an inexpensive way to start marketing your services. If you have the use of a computer at home or school, creating a handbill will be easier and less costly. If no computer is available, use a typewriter or print with a template. Some libraries have typewriters for public use, and there is usually no charge. Make a rough draft of the handbill so you can see how your flyer will look. At the top, put your name and telephone number. If you are using graphics or a template, be sure the telephone number is large enough to be seen easily. You may want to repeat it at the bottom. Think of a catchy title like: HAVE MUSCLE, WILL TRAVEL, or NO JOB TOO BIG OR TOO SMALL. You may want to give your company a name like: "Errands, Ink," or use your own name, "Jane/John Doe & Associates" (even before you actually have any associates). Having a partner may also be something to consider, especially for larger jobs and back-up.

If you are artistic, add art work showing figures in action: washing windows, baby sitting, or repairing a chair. If your talents lie in directions other than art, use comic strip characters. Dagwood mowing the lawn or Gordo's housekeeper dusting are two examples that will add a nice touch. Arrange them on the paper for copying later. Look through the comics for ideas.

Now add your list of services. You must decide whether or not to put prices on the handbill. Do you want to negotiate prices for each job? Do you want to set different rates for each task? Do you want to start out with a simple "per hour" rate? Think about it.

Now, look over your draft carefully. How is the lay-out? It should not be cluttered. Is the text balanced on the page? Are all the words spelled correctly? Do not let the dictionary be a stranger; it is a great tool. This handbill is going to be your "calling card." It must look as professional as possible. You will be judged by its appearance. The better it looks, the more confidence your prospective clients will have in hiring you. The handbill does not have to be expensive; however, it should be neat and well thought out.

Have the bills printed at a local copy shop. Check around for prices. Copies can range anywhere from 3 cents to 10 cents per copy, or even more, depending on quantity and where you go for them.

Marketing—After your copies are made, place them on local bulletin boards, at clubs, churches, nursing homes, retirement centers, shopping malls, and supermarkets. Give them to parents of friends. Talk to managers of apartment buildings and condos. The manager may allow you to put your notice on the bulletin board, in the social center, or in the laundry room. Put your flyers on car windshields and any other place where you think people will see them. If there are businesses nearby, place handbills on employees' cars, but ask permission first. The owner may allow you to use the company bulletin board. These people may really need help. Always carry a supply of your hand bills; you never know when you will run into a prospective client.

Real estate brokers know about residents and businesses who are moving in and out of homes and offices every day. These people may need assistance with clean-up, packing, or with the actual move. They may be delighted to see you.

Now, you can sit back and wait for the telephone calls, right? Wrong. You must be ready for your public. Practice what you will say when these people call. Think of questions they might ask about your background; after all, they will be trusting you with their house, car, child or possessions. Speak clearly and courteously. Sound confident, but not arrogant. Be yourself. Only commit to what you can realistically do for these prospective clients. Be there on time, or let them know if you are running late. A telephone call is always appreciated and may smooth ruffled feathers.

Make a simple work order form on 3" x 5" cards so that you will have a record of your customers. Get as much information on these cards as possible: name, address, phone, type of job, and rate. When business slows down, these cards will be your sales leads. Also use a calendar with large squares for bookings. Refer to it when making an appointment and log in the time and estimated length of the job. Keep it by the phone.

Communicate—Make every effort to understand what your client wants and advise him what you intend to do. Surprises are no fun for anyone. Consider putting your proposed work in writing.

Dress appropriately for the job. Jeans and tennies are perfect for chores around the house or warehouse, but not for accompanying someone downtown, or for working in an office. No matter what clothing is worn, be neat and clean, with hair trimmed, shoes shined, and nails that are clean and filed.

Whatever the job, do your very best. You will be building a reputation, either a good one or a bad one. Word of mouth is the kind of advertising money cannot buy. If you do the best job you can, soon you will be so busy that you will be raising your rates or hiring a staff, or both!

Not So Big

Adhesive tape removal can be accomplished easily by rubbing baby oil or vegetable oil on the tape and surrounding area. Voila! No more tears or smarting. If you must use adhesive tape over a long period of time, there is a product that can relieve skin irritation. It is Tegaderm, made by 3M. It is applied to the skin and the tape is placed over it. It stays in place when the tape is removed. The reason that it is not irritating to the skin is because it "breathes."

Blisters—Help prevent irritation from new shoes. Place adhesive tape inside the heel area (counter) until the shoes are broken in.

Dividing anything can be a problem—Who gets the biggest share? Whether it is a chore, a sandwich, or a treat. It does not have to be a problem for King Solomon. Just try this simple method that should please both kids. One child divides, and the other child chooses. What could be more fair?

Hallowe'en in July—Next time your children cannot think of a single fun thing to do on a summer day, drag out all those old Hallowe'en costumes. The neighbor children can join in the fun too. If no costumes are available, panel curtains make interesting costumes. Add some old hats, belts, scarves and for the girls, purses and jewelry. What about having a parade with a wagon as a float?

Set up a camp in the back yard—If you do not have a tent, give the kids an old sheet, or bedspread. An Army blanket will also work well. They can pretend they are far away from civilization and must fend for themselves. They can make a fishing rod to "catch fish," and forage for fruits and vegetables. Exploring the territory, and looking for buried treasure are other activities that will stimulate their imagination.

Play country store—The children can make most everything to set-up their "market." You can get them started by helping to draw paper money and they can cut it out. Perhaps you have an old board game that has play money. Use buttons for change. Give the kids nearly empty cereal and soap containers. (Place the contents in covered jars). The kids can make pictures of fruit, candy, canned goods, and other products to stock their store. They can give the store a name and make SALE signs.

Latchkey kids—Back-up supervision and transportation is sometimes needed for children of single parents or where both parents work. Hire a reliable, neighborhood mother to cover the times and appointments that conflict with your schedule. Establish specific, mutually agreed upon hours, conditions, and rules. Pay her by the hour and by the trip. Just knowing she is available will make your life easier at your place of employment.

Party balloons—Put small prizes in large balloons before they are blown up; anything that will fit in the nozzle (you can stretch it somewhat). Little surprises like coins, lapel pins, charms, or figures (only smooth items, because you do not want to burst your "bubble"). Some items can be wrapped in tissue and placed in a small container, such as a miniature jar or empty prescription container. Place the mouth of the balloon over the container and invert, the surprise will then fall inside the balloon. When you remove the container from the balloon nozzle, you will be ready to inflate. Give the balloons as prizes or favors. You can add a little mystery to your party by using balloons as holders for directions to a treasure hunt—giving each player a different clue.

Rainy day fun—Add some sunshine to a rainy afternoon. The children can make a floor plan of the interior of a house using a large piece of cardboard. This can be the large side cut from a carton and used as the base. Perhaps you can get them started.

Make the rooms large enough to hold pictures of furniture from a mail order catalog such as the Sears book. The children can go "shopping" until they find enough items to fill each room with furniture, carpeting and drapes.

They can also choose a "family" to live in their new house and cut out clothing with tabs to hold them in place. Outside the house they may want a swimming pool, patio, umbrella, gym set, hedge, and flowers. After everything has been arranged just the way they want it, all the pieces can be pasted in place. The children can make their own paste with a little flour to which is added a small amount of salt and water. The water should be added very slowly, if it is too soupy, add a little more flour. Stir the mixture and you have glue. They can apply it with a popsicle stick or spoon handle.

If you want to "redecorate," carefully remove the pasted items, or glue on a new floor covering over the old room so you can start all over. Look through old magazines for food, autos, or any items not found in the catalog. Perhaps the children would like to draw some of the items such as a fireplace, a dog, or treehouse.

Another rainy day activity—Save all those birthday cards with animals on the covers for a circus train. If the children need more animals, they can look through magazines or draw their own. They can cut out each animal and paste it on the center of a paper. On a separate paper, they can draw a cage large enough to hold the paper animal. Then they can make two spoked wheels and several bars to paste on later. The wheels can be made by placing a plastic drinking glass, upside down, on the paper and drawing around it. They can use a ruler to help draw the spokes, to measure the length of the bars, and to actually draw the bars. Now, they can put their friend in his new cage and paste on the bars and two wheels. The bars should be far enough apart so that the animal can see out and be seen. After the cages are completed for all the animals, connect the cages with yarn or ribbon and the circus train is finished. You may want to help hang it on the child's bedroom wall.

Set up a small tent and play summer—Have a picnic lunch. Allow your children to invite their stuffed toys. If the kids are good, perhaps you will let them spend the night in the tent.

If no tent is available, stretch a sheet between twin beds or a bed and dresser.

Make your own thank-you notes—When people give your children presents, one way to repay the thoughtfulness is to help the tots make cards to show their appreciation. Fold a piece of 8-½" by 11" paper in half and then in half again. Use any color paper you like. Look through old magazines for pretty flowers, animals, or something of interest, such as baseball, swimming, or cars. When they find something they really like, have them cut it out and paste it on the cover of the hand-made card. Perhaps they would rather make a drawing for the cover. Another source for the cover is old birthday cards. Let the kids cut out the part they like and paste it on the cover of their card. Inside the card they can add a smaller, matching design. If they use a flower on the cover, they can use a smaller flower on the inside.

Help them write a note mentioning the gift. This is one way they can express how grateful they are. It will surely be treasured by the receiver, knowing they took time out to make something special.

Toys—After birthdays and Christmas holidays there are so many new toys. Hide a few for restless days and for auto trips. Rotate the toys and your child can enjoy them all over again.

Remnants from the lumber yard make constructive toys. Be sure they are smooth and store them in large string bags, such as potato bags.

Large toilet tissue cartons or appliance boxes are great fun and have so many uses. Just use your imagination.

1. Make a camp in the back yard. Open the carton to make walls. Use a blanket or sheet for the roof.
2. Rolling around the yard in a large carton can be fun too.

3. Flattened, cartons make great "sleds" on a grassy hill.
4. Create a frontier town with many cartons. Make a sheriffs office, church, school house, barber shop, and hotel. Paint the boxes bright colors, make signs, and paint on doors and windows.
5. Make a spaceship, wagon train, or time machine.
6. Save a large carton for a temporary play pen or crib when friends with babies visit.

Store bath toys in a net onion sack. Hang it on the faucet to drain and store when bathtime is over.

Store beach toys in a net onion bag—Toys will be dry and sand-free if you give the bag a few shakes before returning home.

Gifts for the new baby—When giving a present to an infant, it is also thoughtful to include something for older children so they will not feel left out. If you have a new baby, set aside a few small gifts in case your friends are not so thoughtful.

Babies

Baby's food will stay warm longer if you use an egg poacher for heating and serving. Pour hot water into the bottom section and place the food in the three small, separate containers. Test the food to see that it is the proper temperature before feeding your child. Keep the container out of baby's reach.

Mashed bananas—After your doctor has given you the go ahead on giving your baby this bone building fruit, mash part of a fresh banana with a fork. It is less costly and more nourishing then canned bananas.

A pillow case makes a perfect bassinet sheet—

Place a flannel diaper (tucked in securely) over the area where baby's head will rest. If he drools, spits up or sheds hair, it is easy to replace the diaper with a clean one without changing the whole cover.

Cold climates—Protect baby from cold air and drafts by placing newspapers under the mattress (on top of the springs). Do not put the crib near an outside wall. If it must be located on an outside wall, cover it with cardboard or plywood. Use bumper pads around the crib to protect the baby from crib rails. This also helps keep drafts away. Put baby in a warm, blanket, zipper bag to insure him staying covered at night. Dress him in the same weight clothing throughout the season. Make sure the shirts and sleepers are all the same weight. Switching could cause a cold. If you cannot keep the window open at night, air the room thoroughly during the day while baby is in another part of the house.

Diaper rash—Put baking soda in a salt shaker and use it sparingly on baby's bottom. Carefully wash baby with each diaper change and then sprinkle the baking soda on the irritated area. By using baking soda regularly, and changing diapers often, you may never have a diaper rash problem. If a bad rash does develop, try this: brown ½ cup of flour in a pan. Pour it in a shaker and apply to baby's bottom after each diaper change.

Receiving blankets make excellent night diapers for older babies and untrained toddlers. Fold the blanket "kite" shaped, and line it with a rectangular folded diaper. Cover with plastic pants. For older children, a piece of soft plastic can be pinned directly to the diaper.

If cutting baby's fingernails is a traumatic experience for you both, do the trimming while the infant is relaxed and asleep.

When buying furniture for a young child, keep

in mind that he is growing very fast. He will not stay little very long and buying furniture is a big investment. Unless you intend to pass this furniture on to a younger sibling, buy a bed, dresser, and desk that will still fit him as he matures. Choose floor, bed and wall coverings that are appropriate for him now. Instead of changing the furnishings, change these less expensive items as his tastes and needs change. The basic pieces of furniture will still serve him even as an adult.

Safety pins will penetrate diapers and other fabrics easily if you first stick the pin into a bar of soap. Carefully running the pin through your hair is another way. The electricity in your tresses does the trick.

Child-proof your home before your baby is big enough to start exploring. Dispose of guns. Lock up medications, chemicals, and any other potentially dangerous substances. Attach an accordion gate to the kitchen door and all stairways. Never back the car out of the garage or driveway until you know exactly where your child is. Inspect your home for any dangerous materials or areas that could harm your child.

Eliminate sour odors—Keep baking soda on hand. If baby spits up, this dry substance will neutralize the sour smell. When away from home keep a small container of baking soda in your diaper bag.

Direct sunlight is not good for your infant's sensitive eyes. A protective bonnet will help. Covering his head with a light blanket whenever he is in bright sunshine will assure no exposure to direct light. Your child should wear sun glasses as soon as possible. It may preserve his vision so that he will never need eye glasses in later life. Keep in mind that blue eyes are more sensitive to light than brown eyes.

CHAPTER 12

Just for Pets

Even finicky cats may eat brands of food they do not like if you mix in a little canned tuna fish.

"Train" your cat to keep off of certain areas such as on chairs, counter tops, carpets, etc. Put pieces of orange rind in these off limit zones. Cats hate this citrus aroma. Try this for two or three weeks and see if your feline gets the message. You may get the animal to stop clawing furniture by using this same method.

According to many vets, flea collars are poisonous to animals. So what can you do to rid your dog of these irritating and persistent critters? Here is an alternative flea deterrent. Bathe your canine in a solution of one capful of Avon's Skin-So-Soft added to a tub full of water. Fleas hate it. Do not try this on cats, they may be too sensitive to the odor.

Other flea relief solutions for "hot spot" flea bites are:

1. Bag Balm is a mild, but effective salve. It was originally used by farmers for infected cow udders. Bag Balm can be used daily and is available at health food stores. Many meat cutters use this for their own cuts and infections.

2. Black tea, prepared as you would for drinking may be applied to the area with cotton several times a day.

3. Fleas do not like brewer's yeast. Pat the powder on your dog's coat and he will be flea-free!

Kitty litter odors—Add one part borax to six parts litter mix to help the box stay fresh longer.

Locate your pet with a keyfinder—Place this electronic key keeper on your animal's collar and find him the same way you would locate those evasive keys, by simply clapping your hands.

Make moving to a new home safe for your feline—Do not wash the cat's belongings before the move.

His best sense is *smell*. Keep him in a carrier the day of the move. All that activity can be frightening; he may even run away. When you arrive at the new house, keep him in one room surrounded by his blanket, bed, scratching post, or toys. Anything that has a familiar scent will make the move less traumatic and help him to feel comfortable sooner. Keep him indoors for a week or two so that he can familiarize himself with his new home. Take him out on a leash at first, so he can get his bearings in the neighborhood. He may have trouble finding his way home if he is alone, because he goes more by scent than vision. He is now the "new cat" on the block and he may have a territorial fight with another cat. He must be able to find his way home if this happens. So prepare him for his new environment before you turn him loose.

Give your dog a dry shampoo bath in winter— Sprinkle baking soda over his coat and rub into his body. Brush thoroughly. He will be cleaner and smell fresh.

CHAPTER 13

Just for the Car

Batteries

Deter battery theft—Outside hood release latches can tempt battery theft. Purchase a padlock and a piece of steel chain long enough to secure the hood of your car. This is a nuisance, but may prevent costly and time-consuming loss of your car battery. Often when a battery is stolen, the thief returns a few nights later and steals the new one!

Corrosion prevention for your car battery. Cover the cable terminals with petroleum jelly. If they are already corroded, remove the terminals from their posts and thoroughly clean with a solution of baking soda and water. WIPE ABSOLUTELY DRY BEFORE RECONNECTING.

Cleaning

Car washing during freezing weather—After washing your car do not lock the doors for at least four hours. There may be water in the locks that can freeze. **If the lock is frozen**, heat the key with a match before inserting it into the lock. Be sure to wipe inside edges of doors after running through the car wash. This will help prevent car doors from freezing shut.

Splatters and road grime can be removed with dry baking soda on a damp cloth. Wipe windshields, headlights, chrome, and paint and rinse with clear water.

A clean steering wheel—Keep a box of moist towelettes in the car to freshen the wheel in between car washes. They will also come in handy for wipe ups when no water is available.

Tar and oil stains can be removed from fenders by saturating a cloth with baby oil and rubbing the soiled area. Another method is to use any carbonated cola drink. Dampen a cloth with the cola and rub it into the oil and tar. This is the best use of cola that I can think of; it certainly beats drinking it and is much healthier for your liver.

Washing your car—Use a gentle detergent and warm water. Start with the roof and work down. If the car is very dirty, hose it off first. After washing and rinsing, dry it with soft towels. Start with the windows, then do the chrome, and finally, do the body (starting again with the top and working down). By the time you get to the body the towel will be damp, which will help remove any water spots or streaks.

Waxing your vehicle—Always do it in a shaded area.

Oil drips in the driveway or in the garage—Pour baking soda over the oily area. Leave it there overnight to absorb the oil, then sweep it up and put it in the garbage can where it will absorb odors there. Place a large piece of cardboard or plywood over the area where your car drips oil.

On the Road

Running out of gas is bad enough, but after you return from the station with a gallon of fuel, your car still may not start. Pour all but one half cup of gas into your tank. Save this small portion to prime the carburetor. If the engine will not start, turn the starting switch off and remove the keys. Open the hood and remove the air filter; it is fastened with a wing nut. Pour about two tablespoons of the remaining fuel directly into the carburetor opening. Replace the filter before trying to start the engine. You may have to do this twice before the engine will keep running. DO NOT LET ANYONE TRY TO START THE ENGINE WHILE YOU ARE POURING THE GAS-OLINE INTO THE CARBURETOR.

Joining an auto club is probably one of the best investments you can make, not only for yourself, but if you have children that drive, or are passengers in cars of friends, you will feel safer knowing the Auto Club is always there to help.

Have you ever been late or missed work because your car wanted the day off?—Before this happens, make arrangements with a co-worker who lives in the vicinity to trade rides whenever one of you is car-less.

Engine overheating can happen in heavy traffic when you are going no place fast. Put the transmission in neutral whenever you stop so the fan can help cool the engine. Turn off the air conditioning so the engine will not have to work so hard. If the car is still overheating pull off the road, leave the engine running, set the hand brake, put it in neutral, and raise the hood to allow the car to cool. If you stop the engine, the water stops circulating and may cause boiling. Do not remove the radiator cap as this will reduce the pressure and could also cause boiling, or an accidental burn. The car should be okay within a half hour, but go to the nearest service station and have it checked.

Parking your car will be easier with this bit of advice. If there is a glass store front where you park, use the reflection of your car, as you back in, to judge how close you are to the auto behind.

Storage

Store the garden hose in the trunk of your car

if you are short of space. This is especially convenient for apartment and condo dwellers. The hose will be readily available for that next car wash. After each use, wipe it with the wet rag you used to wash the car. Do this as you roll up the hose, draining as much water as possible. Fasten both ends together before storing, this will prevent leakage onto your trunk.

Store other items in the trunk of your car—If you have limited storage space in your home or apartment, keep large, but light weight, bulky items like bottled water, toilet tissue, and paper towels in the trunk. This might also allow you to take advantage of sales you would otherwise not consider because of space restrictions.

CHAPTER 14

Mind Your Own Business

Book Purchases

Save on multiple book purchases—Is there a favorite book you enjoyed and want to share with others? Perhaps a book you would like to give to several friends for Christmas. Go to the library and look in *Books in Print* for the publisher and buy directly from him. You may be able to reduce the price by 40% if you purchase at least 3 copies. Always ask.

Classified Shopping

Shopping in the classified ads—If there is no urgency for the item you wish to purchase, try this: Start watching the classified section of your daily newspaper for those products that interest you. As an example, let us assume you wish to buy a used computer. Write down the phone number of each ad that sounds good. Keep watching the ads daily. When the ad is no longer listed, call the number. If the computer has been sold you are out of luck, but if the advertiser just got tired of spending money on his ad, you could be the lucky one. Offer the seller less than the advertised price; he may be ready to reduce his profit by now. There are many new computers sitting on closet shelves, some still in their original cartons, because the owners did not get around to learning how to use them. This method of shopping can be used for any classified ad product, when it is a buyer's market and you have the time to pursue it.

Computers and Printers

Computer disk files—Print out the menu of each

disk and cut it out so it will fit inside the disk envelope. Update as you enlarge the files. This will aid in searching for a file without having to go through each menu. When the disk is full, or no further changes are needed, print a copy and glue it to the *outside* of the disk holder or use it as a label by placing it directly on the disk. Another simple filing method is to number each disk, print out the menus, specifying the number of the disk and place it in alphabetical order, by subject, into a notebook for easy reference. Update as needed.

Catch more mistakes when proofreading— Read backwards. If you peruse from the right hand side of the page or screen, it will slow you down enough to look at each letter instead of skimming the page.

Never look at the computer screen for more than three hours at one time. Keep an eye on the clock and take a fifteen minute break to rest your eyes.

Economical Computer Printer Ribbons—
National Computer Ribbons
9562 Deerco Road
Timonium, Maryland 21093
1-800-292-6272

They carry and manufacture many compatible computer ribbons. I was delighted with their prices, quality, service and attitude. This is a sample of what is available:

Brand	What I was paying	Their price
Brother XL	$6-8	$4.50
IBM Proprinter XL	$11-13	$4.50
IBM Graphics	$7-8	$2.50

It is necessary to purchase at least six ribbons, but they do not need to be the same kind. Perhaps you can ask a friend to order with you. The ribbons arrived promptly and worked as well as the previous, more costly ones I had purchased in the past. That 800 number is an added bonus. Some ribbons, such as the IBM Quietwriter, are only available at the manufacturer's price.

Save paper—Use the clean side of used 8-1/2" by 11" paper for file or first draft copies. (Draw a diagonal line through the used side). Many advertisements received in the mail are only printed on one side. Save it for your scrap paper file. Save other sources of paper such as spoiled letter head, or paper from old files. This scrap paper can also be used to make note pads. Cut it in fourths or sixths, stack and staple.

Erasers

Clean dirty, rubber, pencil or pen erasers by rubbing them against an emery board, nail file, or sandpaper.

Felt Pens

Extend the life of felt pens—When the writing becomes faint or the pen runs dry, add a little water or few drops of matching food coloring. This is done by removing the cap on the opposite end from the tip. (You may need to use pliers). Add the liquid and replace the cap. It might not be as good as new, but it will add life of your pen.

Felt pens will write better and longer if you store them point down. This will prevent the ink from running away from the writing tip.

Job Interview Tips

Just like the Boy Scouts, you must be pre-pared—Here are four things to give you a leading edge during your interview and help land the job:

1. **Do your homework**—Find out all you can about the company. Make a trip to the library and do research. Learn about their products, history, top management, and services. Use this information in conversation during the meeting. The interviewer will have to be impressed.

2. **Be enthusiastic** about the company and the position itself. Practice in your mind what you will say. What questions might come up. How your background makes you desirable for this position. What kind of a contribution can you make personally. Use your imagination.

3. **Get there on time**. Make a dry run if the meeting will be held in an unfamiliar area. Allow adequate time to arrive feeling relaxed. Consider traffic flow and parking at the appointed hour of interview.

4. **Be a good salesperson**. We are all salespeople, one way or another. So sell yourself first before asking, "What can the company do for me?" However, this is also an important consideration.

Lost or Found Something?

There is now a toll free number to call that lists lost and found items throughout the entire country. If you have found something, the call is free. If you are looking for a lost item, you will be charged $15 (billed to your credit card) to list it with the service. Call 1-800-828-3463.

Reading

So many things arrive in the mail that you would like to go over more thoroughly: catalogs, books, offers, but there is never enough time. You either toss them upon arrival or store them with good intentions and then end up throwing them away later, without ever reading them. Here is an alternative: Keep all those interesting catalogs and sales pitches next to your favorite TV chair. When a commercial comes on the TV, you can do your own commercial reading.

Mailing

Protect return and consignee address labels— Cover them with transparent tape to ensure they stay in place until the letter or package reaches its destination.

Protect outgoing mail from rain—Place it in *two* plastic bags. When you reach the mail box, remove the first one, which may be wet. Leave the second plastic bag on as you post the letters. This will protect them from other mail that may not be dry.

Address envelopes before applying postage—If you make an error you will only have wasted an envelope.

Recycle large envelopes received in the mail. First, remove the address label and stamps. Cut a small strip along the two sides and turn inside out. You now have a fresh looking envelope to mail books, tapes, or anything that will not fit in a regular legal size envelope.

Speed up outgoing mail—If there is a government installation, such as a military base, post, hospital, or office, nearby, mail your letters from there. The Post Office gives them priority service. Our local second class Post Office has two pick-ups daily. The government complex, just two blocks away, has five pick-ups each week day. Be sure to check the notice on the box for the current schedule.

Return Labels

If you have a small or part-time business, but no mailing labels, order inexpensive personal return labels. Instead of your own name, have them imprinted with your company name. Even though you may have letterhead envelopes, these labels can be used on packages and bills with their own return envelope. These handy stickers may also be used on plain envelopes when it is not necessary to waste your printed business envelopes. There is usually an ad to purchase them in the coupon section of the Sunday paper and the cost is sometimes as low as $2 per 1,000 labels.

When ordering from a mail order catalog, insure legibility, and save time, by using a personalized address label on the order form.

When ordering anything by mail, always write down the name and address of the company, date ordered, items, and price. Save it until the merchandise arrives. This information may be valuable if you do not hear from the supplier. It is a law that mail order companies must ship within six weeks or give you the option of cancelling the order. A good place to note this information is on a calendar. Put it on the date that is six weeks into the future. Then you will not need to remember the date you ordered the merchandise.

Newspapers

Preserve newspaper articles—To one quart of club soda, add one milk of magnesia tablet. Mix well and freeze overnight. Thaw and pour into a flat pan, large enough to soak the newspaper article. After one hour, remove the paper and dry flat. This will preserve the paper and prevent it from yellowing. Before you try this on an original article, experiment with a sample of the paper to make sure you do it correctly.

Paying Bills

Bank at a financial institution that pays interest on checking accounts. Write checks to pay bills, but do not mail them until it is near the due date. Allow enough time for the check to arrive at its destination before the due date. In the meantime, keep the envelopes containing your bills in a safe place where you will be reminded to mail them. Write the mailing date in the upper right hand corner of each envelope. This will be covered by the stamp later. Your money will stay in your account longer collecting interest. This can be a significant amount over time.

Photos

Protect picture developing by placing a label with your name and address on the finished roll of film before taking it to be developed. Use a printed return address label and secure it with a piece of transparent tape. This will help prevent the pictures from being lost or given to the wrong person, if they become separated from their envelope.

Write on the back of photos by applying file folder labels. Write on the label instead of directly on the photo back. Photo paper does not absorb the ink and may run on the front of other photos.

Taxes

Throughout the year keep a tax folder in an accessible place. Each time you have a tax related purchase or expenditure, such as a visit to a physician or dentist, buy a medical appliance, pay your property tax, take out an IRA, or make a stock market transaction, put the receipt or a note in this folder. If you are not sure it is tax deductible, save it anyway. Later you can check with an accountant or tax consultant. This will save you time when preparing taxes and help capture expenses that may be forgotten later.

Telephone

Keep a record of all telephone calls—Place a steno pad by the phone. Write down outgoing as well as incoming calls. Record the date, telephone number, person, and subject. This tablet can become invaluable when doing taxes: when you bought or sold a stock, or called the IRS for information; when you are trying to remember who did such a good job cleaning the carpet, or fixing that leaky faucet. It also gives you a record to check against the telephone bill when it arrives with many more long distance calls than you remember placing. When the book is full, label it with the dates included, file the book and start a new one. If you use this steno pad faithfully it can be a very valuable tool that you will come to rely on.

Emergency telephone numbers will always be available if you type or print a list of the numbers and attach it to the bottom of each telephone in your home. Use transparent tape to fasten them securely.

Telephone directories can be purchased for any city, town or hamlet in the US for under $25. The smaller the book, the less costly. Perhaps you would like a current book of your old home town or a copy of the directory where you do business. The Pacific Bell Telephone Company provides this service. Just call 1-800-848-8000 and they will tell you how it works. A telephone directory might make an unusual, but appropriate gift for the person who has everything.

Obscene telephone calls are very upsetting. Keep a whistle near the telephone. if you receive one of these distressing calls, blow the whistle loudly into the mouthpiece and then quickly hang up. The caller is not likely to bother you again and may even think twice before calling anyone else.

Three Hole Punched Paper

Three hole punched paper will last longer and be stronger if you place a piece of folded transparent tape where the hole is and repunch it. Also do this to paper holes that need repair.

Warranties On Appliances

Place appliance warranties and instruction

manuals in a clear plastic bag and store them in a
kitchen drawer or on a closet shelf. If you have many,
alphabetize them by appliance such as "fan", "hair
dryer", "iron", "mixer", "stereo", or "TV" for quick
reference.

Work or Play Surface

A formica counter top with back board can be
purchased from a hardware or lumber supply house.
They come in different lengths and can be placed on
two-drawer file cabinets or connected to the wall with
angle brackets. This very durable surface can be used in
a home office for a desk or computer table, in a child's
room for play and toy storage, or for a student study
area. Best of all the price is right. A six foot piece is
under $25.

CHAPTER 15

Here & There

Diet

Eating in the evening—If you cannot seem to stop raiding the refrigerator in the evening, try this: Dab a little garlic oil under your nose. It should take away any desire to eat! You may want to do this when you are alone. Wash off the garlic when you retire.

Diminish hunger pangs by doing 10 or 15 sit ups. This reduces the flow of acids to the stomach, which is the source of feeling hungry.

Give up dinner to lose weight—You will then burn up the day's calories before retiring. Eat breakfast and put off lunch until two or three in the afternoon. Make sure you get at least 70 grams of protein, plus fruit and vegetables in these two meals. If you should get hungry, have a glass of non-fat milk before going to bed.

Eat less at mealtime by being relaxed—Play pleasant, relaxing music while you dine. This will reduce your stress level and may help you to eat less; chew your food more slowly; take longer to eat; and feel more satisfied.

Cut calories by using lettuce in place of bread for a sandwich. Try different varieties of lettuce such as romaine, Australian, or red leaf. They are generally more flavorful and nutritious than the standard head, or iceberg type.

Lose weight by cutting down—Eat only half as much as you would normally eat, without changing your diet. For example: if you usually eat one slice of bread, eat only ½ slice. Try eating only half of a baked potato instead of the entire spud. You probably will not miss the food, but you will notice the weight loss.

If you can tolerate the taste, chew your vitamins before swallowing them—You will assimilate them more quickly. Do not chew acidic vitamins such as niacin, vitamin C, potassium or hydrochloric acid.

If you include a B Complex in your vitamins, always take it *after* a meal. Taking it before eating may increase your appetite and give you a feeling of being "wired."

Exercise

Counting laps while swimming can be a nuisance. it is much more enjoyable to concentrate on swimming or even day-dreaming. Try this: Time your laps *once*, then take a timer or alarm clock and set it for the required time and forget it. Be sure the clock is in a safe, dry place. This method may work better in a private, backyard pool, rather than a crowded public one. However, the public pool may have a wall clock.

When walking, jogging, or biking in the rain, or during evening hours, wear bright, or light colored clothing so that you will be visible to drivers and other bikers.

Walking is an excellent form of exercise if done on a regular basis. It is something you can do solo and the only "equipment" needed is a sturdy pair of shoes and heavy socks. If you live in a part of the country that has extreme temperatures, do your walking in a covered or air conditioned mall. If you do it before ten AM, you will not bother shoppers. The stimulation and solitude of walking will help develop great ideas and even solve problems. An added bonus to this easy exercise is it helps alleviate tension while you keep fit.

Eye Protection

Tanning booths can be very dangerous to eyes—If you must use this artificial device, be sure to protect your "peepers" with goggles designed for this purpose.

Speaking of eyes, when you lie in the sun, protect them by putting a cotton ball soaked in witch hazel over your closed lids. Besides protecting your eyes, it is very refreshing.

Help protect your eyes from cataracts—Recent studies show that eyes that are exposed to bright sunlight are more susceptible to this damaging disease. Wearing dark glasses and/or a hat in sunlight can be your insurance for healthy eyes and good vision.

Have Your Own Flea Market

Whether you are planning a garage, yard, patio, or apartment sale a little planning will pay off in big dollars and provide a fun day or weekend.

1. Make a list of anything you want to sell. Go through closets, the attic, garage, and cabinets for ideas. Every time you think of something, add it to your list. Have the entire family list their discards. When it comes time to gather the items, nothing will be overlooked.
2. Prepare a flyer for neighbors, bulletin boards and any place you can post the news of your coming sale.
3. Will it pay to run a classified ad in the local paper? Think about it.
4. Ask your neighbors to join in. If you do, give them

enough notice to prepare. Decide how you will divide the profits ahead of time so there will not be any hard feelings. Will you keep everyone's possessions separate? Will you tag each person's things with a specific colored price marker, for tabulation later?

5. Cut pieces of masking tape for price labels on small items; clothing, toys, books, pictures, and lamps. Use a black felt pen for prices. On larger and expensive items, you may want to make posters or large signs to alert your customers.

6. Make sure you have enough change. Use a covered box or pocketed apron to hold some of the money. Use only enough to make change. Keep the balance in a safe place.

7. Put out a flag or a colorful bunch of balloons to attract people. In the flyer, after the address, say something like: "come to the big balloons" or "watch for the red, white, and blue."

8. Speaking of balloons, mention in your flyer that you are giving away free balloons to children. This will encourage kids to ask their parents to come by.

9. Late in the day, reduce prices on items you do not want to keep.

10. When you are finished with your hopefully successful sale, call a charity to take the articles that remain unsold.

Grocery Shopping

An ice chest can be used for shopping trips in very warm weather or when you do not plan to return home immediately. Do not depend on the chest for frozen foods if you plan to be away for more than an hour. It

will keep perishables cool as long as enough ice remains
and the lid is securely in place.

Prevent grocery bags from spilling while driving
home. Fasten them in seat belts.

Keys

Key reminder—To get in the habit of remember-
ing your house and car keys, try this: Make a key board.
Screw hooks into a nicely finished board. Place it on a
wall nearest the outside door that is used most often
(front, back, or garage door). All family members can
drop their keys off when returning home. The key board
will help remind everyone to pickup their keys on the
way out. The key board can be built into the form of a
wall hanging box with a cover. If you construct one
yourself, choose a nice piece of wood and shellac it. You
may want to use plywood and paint or cover it with
contact or wall paper. If you are creative, paint a picture on it to match the decor of the room where it will
hang. Perhaps you would rather purchase one.

Prevent an expensive locksmith visit—Have a
house key hidden in the yard, shed, or garage. Make
sure it will not be discovered by the wrong person by
placing it in an obscure place. Trade keys with someone you trust in the neighborhood. Keep a house key in
your car.

Miscellaneous

**Keep a record in your address book of part
numbers** such as for the vacuum cleaner bag, battery
sizes or any other items you use regularly. When you

are out shopping you will have the number handy for replacement.

Port & Starboard for the infrequent sailor. You will never forget these two nautical terms if you remember this: *Port* is *left*, both words are short and *Starboard* is *right*, both words are longer.

Safety at Traffic Lights

Traffic lights—Whether you are driving a car or are a pedestrian, use the "3 second" rule. When the light changes to green, look both ways before crossing. This will give you the 3 second delay and will protect you somewhat from people who run lights. Most intersection accidents happen when the signal is with the injured. This little pause is very effective while travelling in England, where Americans instinctively look the wrong way first, before crossing.

CHAPTER 16

Moving

Moving day can be exhausting—Here are a few tips that will make your relocation a little easier for everyone.

1. Plan ahead. As soon as you know you are moving, make a time table. List everything that needs to be done and when. Here are some samples:
   a) Obtain at least four moving bids, or arrange for a truck.
   b) Hire help. (Who will do the heavy lifting? Who will mind the children?)
   c) Notify present utilities, paper, and phone for shut-off date.
   d) Notify future utilities, paper, and phone for start date.
   e) Advise school to transfer records.
   f) Send out change of address notices or call friends, magazines, banks, investment houses, credit cards, and department stores. As you receive mail each day, use the letters, catalogs, and magazines as a reminder and send a card. Keep a log to prevent duplication.
   g) Gather packing boxes and packing material.
   h) Pack non-essentials such as seasonal clothing, good china, silver, pictures and books ahead of time.
   i) Contact your insurance company to find out if you have coverage during a move. No use to duplicate coverage with the moving company.

2. Now that you are armed with your list, here are some additional suggestions to consider:
   a) Call the Goodwill or Salvation Army for help. They have people who want to work. The rates are reasonable.

b) Every time you make a trip to your new house (if a local move), do not go empty handed. If you take friends to see your new abode, entice everyone to carry something. Maybe you can get them to load up their car, as well as your own.

c) Plants should be taken separately, not in the truck. Take cleaning material, rags, shelf paper, scissors, and a bucket.

d) Be sure you have plenty of newspapers, but remember, the print rubs off, so dishes will need washing before storing.

e) Have tools such as a screw driver, hammer, tape measure, and pliers at the new place as well as the old location.

f) Move anything that is fragile. Lamps and pictures may even be hung in the new home. If not, they should be carefully stored there. You may need help with heavy items.

g) Liquor stores are a good source for obtaining packing boxes. These cartons are sturdy because they originally held heavy glass bottles. They also have dividers that can be used for breakables. Open both ends of boxes so they can be stored flat until needed. Assemble the cartons with masking tape as you pack.

h) Special packing material for mirrors, glass, and lamp shades are available at your local U-Haul company. They also sell blank newsprint for print-free wrapping.

i) Use smaller cartons for heavy items such as tools, books, and small appliances. Use larger cartons for linens, pots and pans, toys, and other light-weight items.

3. When you start packing, write on each cartons with

a heavy, black marking pen to designate for which room it is intended. On some of the boxes you may want to write more than just the room. For instance, on the carton marked "kitchen," you may want to add "everyday dishes," or "perishables, refrigerate immediately." A box marked "Bedroom, clean sheets" will save much time hunting when you are tired and must make beds.

4. Start packing non-essentials early. The attic, basement and garage are all good places to begin. As you progress, and moving day nears, keep out only enough possessions to get by such as: one change of clothing for each member of the family, a few dishes, flatware, pans, and towels, medications, and vitamins.

5. Remove closet clothing from garment bags. The bags are too fragile to withstand the move filled with heavy clothing. Place them in the bottom of the cardboard wardrobes furnished by the moving company.

6. Flammables such as aerosol spray cans, gasoline, and paints, cannot be transported in the moving truck, they are too hazardous. They must be moved in your car.

7. Protect mattresses and pillows. During the move leave fitted sheets on mattresses and cases on pillows. Change them *after* the move.

8. Insure that your new home is insect free. Use bug bombs or have your new house sprayed professionally a week or so before moving in, so the odor will

dissipate. It is so much easier, and better for your family's health, to do this job when the house is empty.

9. Let the upholstery cleaners help with the move. If you are moving locally, send out the living room furniture to be cleaned. Have it returned to the new house.

10. Fasteners will be handy when you are ready to rehang pictures if you tape them to the back of the pictures with masking tape.

11. Long-distance moves. Contact the Chamber of Commerce in your new town. Ask for information about schools, clubs, businesses, stores, parks, museums, physicians, dentists, and anything else that may interest you. Subscribe to the local newspaper—it will answer many questions and give you a "feel" for your new area.

12. Use a large accordion-type envelope for all papers associated with the move. Inside, have two or three legal sized envelopes. On the outside of one, write all contact telephone numbers such as real estate agent, carpet salesman, utilities, post office, etc. Use one envelope for expense receipts; this will be invaluable at tax time. Use another envelope for business cards and contacts. Another can be used for measurements of windows, floors, etc. Keep this portfolio with you as much as possible, it will save time.

13. Complete as many chores as possible at your new home before the move. Anything that can be done

ahead of time will help. Clean the bathrooms and
kitchen appliances, place shelf paper in all cabinets
and closet shelves. Paint and install new carpeting.
Doing this will be much easier while the rooms ar
empty.

CHAPTER 17

Selling a House

Getting Your House Ready

These tips can add value to your home and make it more saleable.

1. The entry should be clean, with an inviting door mat, and attractive plants. This is the prospective buyer's first impression of your home. Do not turn him off before he even gets inside.

2. Play music. Not too loudly. Something tranquil, such as light classical sets a pleasant mood. It encourages the would-be buyer to feel at home, to be comfortable. Maybe want to have it for his very own.

3. Make certain the bathrooms and kitchen are *spotless*. These rooms should shine. No one wants to think about other people's dirt.

4. Do not worry about painting walls unless they are in very poor condition. Most people want to decorate in their own style and color. But do see that walls and woodwork are clean.

5. Put away bric-a-brac, magazines, small appliances and anything else that makes your home look cluttered. Do not have it look too "lived in!" If counters and furniture are relatively empty, it will create a feeling of space. If possible, move some pieces of furniture to the garage or attic if a room looks overcrowded.

6. Show off a bright bouquet of fresh flowers. Use silk flowers in winter and make sure they are fresh and clean.

7. Turn on lights everywhere. Your home should look bright and cheery.

8. Shop around for a real estate agent. Selling your home is very personal and can be traumatic. Make it as easy on yourself as possible. You do not want to have a personality clash. Find an agent that you can communicate with and feel comfortable about.

A Broker's Viewpoint

The following are professional tips from a real estate agency on sprucing up your home.

Let Your Home Smile a Welcome to Buyers:

1. Let the sun shine in. Open draperies and curtains and let the prospect see how cheerful your home can be. (Dark rooms do not appeal).

2. Fix that faucet! Dripping water discolors sinks and suggest faulty plumbing.

3. Safety first. Keep stairways clear. Avoid cluttered appearances and possible injuries.

4. Make closets look bigger. Neat, well ordered closets show that space is ample.

5. Bathrooms help sell homes. Check and repair caulking in bathtubs and showers. Make this room sparkle.

6. Arrange bedrooms neatly. Remove excess furniture. Use attractive bedspreads and freshly laundered curtains.

7. Can you see the light? Illumination is like a welcome sign. The potential buyer will feel a glowing warmth when you turn on your lights for an evening inspection.

When an Agent Shows Your House

1. Three's a crowd. Avoid having too many people present during showings. The potential buyer will feel like an intruder and will hurry through the house.

2. Pets underfoot? Keep them out of the way—preferably out of the house.

3. Silence is golden. Be courteous, but don't force conversation with the potential buyer. He wants to inspect your house—not pay a social call.

4. Be it ever so humble. Never apologize for the appearance of your home. After all, it has been lived in. Let the trained salesman answer any objections. This is his job.

5. Stay in the background. The salesman knows the buyer's requirements and can better emphasize the features of your home when you do not tag along. You will be called if needed.

6. Why put the cart before the horse? Trying to

dispose of furniture and furnishings to the potential buyer before he has purchased the house often loses a sale.

7. A word to the wise. Let your realtor discuss price, terms, possession and other factors with the customer. He is eminently qualified to bring negotiations to a favorable conclusion.

8. Use your agent. Show your home to prospective customers only by appointment, through your agent. Your cooperation will be appreciated and will help close the sale more quickly.

CHAPTER 18

Travel

Planning

Use the library to plan your vacation—There are so many places to consider as a get-away that sometimes it is difficult to make a decision about where to go. Travelling is expensive. What a waste if you do not like your choice! When you are considering vacation spots, first visit your local library and do some research. It can really pay off. Besides sleuthing in books, many libraries have videos that can be checked out and viewed by other members of your family at home on your VCR. Make it a family project, with you as the expert. After all, if they have a hand in the planning and deciding, they will not be able to complain later. When you finish your research you will have a more realistic idea about each considered location. You may also find some fascinating facts about places you had not previously considered.

When preparing for vacation do not forget your feet—See that you have proper walking shoes. Purchase new shoes at least one month before your trip, so that they can be tested and properly broken in. Be sure that your new footwear is large enough. There should be about a quarter of an inch between the end of the shoe and your longest toe. This gives your toes room to spread out when you are walking. Your trip will be more enjoyable with feet that will not let you down.

Lost Luggage

When flying it is a good idea to pack a carry-on bag with essentials—You never know when your baggage will be delayed, or your connecting flight will be cancelled enroute. I learned this the hard way. Once I had to stay in a hotel without even so much as a contact lens case. More recently, I got to the airport without my suitcase! I was headed for Hawaii and there was not enough time to return home for the stray bag. Luckily, I had the essentials in my carry-on, so it was not disastrous. Some things are almost impossible to replace quickly, if at all. Include such necessities as: medication, vitamins, important papers, walking shoes, bathing suit, change of underwear, glasses, and cosmetics. Then, if your luggage takes a different trip than yours, it will not spoil your fun and you will not waste precious time looking for essentials.

Travelling with Children

1. Include the children in the preparation; that is half the fun. Give them their own small case or back pack. Help them select some basics such as: a new toothbrush, paste, sun tan lotion, and dark glasses. Assist them in packing a bathing suit, a few changes of underwear, pjs, socks, and a favorite small toy or game that can be enjoyed in the car. This case should not be too heavy for the child to carry. You will appreciate this case yourself when you are tired and make a motel stop and do not have to rummage through a big suitcase looking for your child's pajamas or fresh underwear.

2. Each day on the road, surprise your child with some new, small toy or game. Things like cards, puzzles, crayons, coloring books, drawing tablets, and story books are all easy to carry and will entertain children throughout the trip. Try to purchase these things on sale well in advance of your vacation.

3. Provide pillows and blankets so your children can be comfortable and able to take a nap, even while being held safely in a seat belt. Stop often so they can be in the fresh air and run and stretch. Remember, children are not in the habit of being still for long periods. It will help them to sit quietly if they have no sugar treats. If a child is in a carseat, take him out frequently to change positions.

4. Pack your own carry-on bag with a change of clothes so it is not necessary to take large bags into a motel at night when you are tired. In the morning, when you are fresh, repack a fresh supply from the bag left in the car trunk.

5. Keep a large plastic bag in the trunk for soiled clothing. They will be ready when you make a laundry stop.

Travelling with Pets

Travelling with a pet—If you have room for your animal's possessions, he will feel more at home, wherever he is. Take his food, dish, leash, collar. Be sure his collar has your full name and address clearly marked. As a temporary name tag for a trip, you can purchase a rugged plastic, baggage tag with a secure fastener.

Miscellaneous

An ice chest can save many dollars on your trip. If you do not have room in your car or if you travel by air, purchase an inexpensive styrofoam ice chest after you arrive at your destination. It will provide cool storage for breakfast (cold cereal, fruit, milk and juice) and make it possible to have other nourishing snacks like cheese, fruit, nuts, yogurt, and beverages. When your trip has ended, you can pass the chest on to someone else along the way. Convenience stores like Seven Eleven usually carry these handy ice chests at a nominal fee. Your first breakfast will more than cover the cost of the ice chest.

Hotel soap is usually made in very thin bars, unless you are stopping at the best hotels. Meld several bars by immersing them in water for a few moments and then press them together and let them dry. After completing your bath or shower, store the soap cake in a soap dish, ashtray, or plastic bag, before the maid has a chance to throw it out or take it home. Collect individually wrapped soap bars throughout your trip and use them when you return home. This will not only be a nice memento of your travels, but also save money.

Save shower caps that some motels and hotels provide. Keep one in the glove compartment of your car, or in your purse for an emergency rain hat.

If you swim, but do not submerge your head, the shower cap will provide a comfortable cover to protect against splashes.

Collect cosmetic and after-shave samples for your travels or for your purse or car. They do not take up much room and will come in handy when you are away from home.

Book matches or hotel cards can be a life saver, especially in a foreign country. Be sure to carry something with the name, address, and telephone number (in the local language) of your temporary residence. If you become lost, any cab driver will get you back to home base.

Taxis—Always ask the fare *before* the trip. Most drivers are honest, but you do not want any unpleasant surprises at your destination. It is always a good idea to ask how much, but it is essential to ask when travelling in a foreign country, even if the route is familiar.

Find interesting and economical items on a trip to a foreign country. Shop in second-hand stores. You may find underpriced jewelry and many other bargains. You will also get a glimpse of the heart of the people by looking through their castoffs.

CHAPTER 19

Yuletide

Wrapping

Create a Christmas "staging" area that the entire family can use. A small corner will do. Set up a card table or desk. Stand rolls of wrapping paper in baskets or waste paper containers. Use several small plastic bowls or baskets for seals, tags, stickers, cards, stamps, return address labels, and ribbon. Make sure there are scissors, pen, transparent tape and an address book.

Make your own ribbon from scraps of fabric. Use pinking shears to give it a pretty, finished appearance. This will also help prevent ravelling. If you do not sew, buy remnants. Look for holiday colors. You do not have to limit the fabric to decorating ribbon. You can also use material to wrap presents.

If you buy presents for many family members and friends, try this to help keep everything organized: Choose one pattern of paper for each family. As an example, for Uncle Joe's family, use Santa decorated paper. For cousin Jane's brood, use a solid green paper and red ribbons. This method will help insure that you gather all the gifts, for each family before you visit, mail, or hand out. It is so disappointing to find stray presents after the festivities are over.

Put a little mystery under your own tree—Use one type of wrapping paper and ribbon for each member of your family. Do not use name tags, but keep a record of the wrapping you used for each person. Paste a swatch of the wrapping on a piece of paper along with the name of the recipient and put it away from curious eyes. This should keep everyone guessing, even the package shakers. You may want to try a simpler method: Give each member of the family a number and use that on a name tag.

Unique name tags—Save Christmas cards you

receive and next year use them for over-sized tags and for decorating packages. Cut off the attractive front cover of cards, fold in half and write inside on the plain surface. For decorating, cut out shapes and glue to wrapping paper or use them for stencils.

Mailing

Save paying tax on presents. Do your gift shopping for out-of-state presents in department stores that do their own shipping. Not only will you save paying sales tax, but you will eliminate standing in long postal or UPS lines to mail the packages. The money you save on tax will probably cover the nominal UPS charges the store collects. Also many stores provide a complimentary gift wrap. Some stores may allow you to enclose in the mailer, other small items you have purchased elsewhere. You must plan ahead and do store shopping early to assure delivery by Christmas.

Applying stamps and sealing Christmas cards or other multiple mailings can be done with little fuss. Put one or two ice cubes on a sponge and place in a shallow dish. Run the stamps and envelopes over the cubes to moisten before applying.

It is traditional to sit down with a cup of coffee and address and stamp holiday cards, but beware! The coffee may prevent the stamp from adhering to the envelope and could fall off before reaching the destination. Try ice cubes instead.

Protect bows when mailing packages by placing a cherry tomato basket over the ribbon. Attach a small piece of transparent tape to hold the bow securely. Clean and save the tomato baskets throughout the year.

Updating records—Save the return address envelope labels on cards you receive. After the holidays update your records and add new addresses of old friends
and addresses of new friends to your Christmas card list.

Decorating

Candles will last longer if you place them in the
refrigerator for several hours before lighting.

**Protect your carpet or floor from tree nee-
dles**—Place a white sheet under the tree. It can also be
the basis for a miniature scene. The sheet will look like
"snowdrifts." You can add small houses, a mirror
"pond," bridge, and figures.

Christmas tree chains—Save the styrofoam "popcorn" bits used for packing material by most department stores. The white pieces can be strung with a
needle and white thread. Drape the chain around your
tree for a festive effect. After the holiday season, store it
in a small box to reuse each year.

Make a natural Christmas wreath—This can be
a fun project for the whole family. Start collecting pine
cones, chestnuts, acorns, and nutshells throughout the
year. Look in the park or on any outings. For the base of
the wreath use a thin piece of plywood, heavy cardboard, or particle board. Cut a circle the size you would
like your wreath to be. Cut a circle in the center to form
a donut. Make a hanger by stapling a soft wire loop to
the back side of the frame. Now place your decorations
around the board. When you are satisfied with the arrangement, glue them in place with rubber cement.
Finish it with a red or green velvet bow and you will
have a beautiful wreath to brighten your door and greet
holiday guests.

Create a wall decoration simply by using a bare tree branch. Spray it white and hang it horizontally. Add artificial birds and small decorations. You can also use it for displaying cards. Hang brightly colored ribbons (about three feet long) from the branches. Pin or staple cards to the ribbons as they are received.

Keep your tree fresh longer by sawing about an inch off the base of the trunk to expose new wood. Then place it outdoors, in a bucket of water, until you are ready to set it up. Buy a stand that has a water holder. This will prevent the tree from drying out so quickly and also reduce the fire hazard.

Living Trees—Consider purchasing a small live tree in a container. This can be located in the house or outdoors, depending on its size. Although the cost may be a little more, it will not be a complete waste after the holidays, like a cut tree. The tree can be planted in your yard. It will also be one more tree that is not cut from our forests.

Decorating without a tree You can still get into the holiday mood without the bother of a Christmas tree. There are many things you can do to make your home festive. Put a string of colored lights around a window or doorway. Use a small ceramic tree that is lighted from within. Place ornaments in a pretty bowl or brandy snifter, and add a velvet ribbon. Hang Christmas cards on strings hung from the ceiling. Place holly or bows on lampshades and mantels. Use lots of scented candles.

Miscellaneous

Directing night visitors to your home—Place a green light bulb in the porch light socket as a beacon to assist first-time guests to your door.

Keep the spirit of Christmas alive while teaching your children to be appreciative of all the time and money that is put into the preparation of their gifts. Let "Santa" fill the stockings, but you take credit for the other gifts. This is a "gift of love," but should not go unappreciated.

Give the gift of caring—For those on your list who have everything or if you do not have the funds to give expensive gifts, put your present in a card. Offer to do something that the person can really use:

1. Water plants while they are on vacation.
2. So many hours of babysitting would be especially welcome to parents.
3. Preparing and delivering a meal might be appreciated by a working mother.
4. Painting a room or working in someone's yard is a nice gift.
5. Wash and wax the car or clean the oven.
6. Teach someone how to use their computer.
7. Use your imagination and you can come up with just the right present and it will show it came from your heart.

A thoughtful thank you note—Take a pictures of family members opening, wearing, or using gifts. Send a picture to the giver when you send a thank you note. A picture *is* worth a thousand words.

Helping your Poinsettia rebloom—At the end of October, put the plant in a very dark closet for thirteen hours and then for eleven hours, put it in the bright light. You must do this daily until the Poinsettia blooms. By the Christmas holidays, it should be in its full splendor. October or November is also a good time to repot last year's plant into a larger container.

Save the left-overs from your Christmas feast—What to do with all that food? Save TV dinner trays. After dinner is over, go around the table and dish up a serving of the main course; turkey, potatoes, vegetables, etc. Place the filled TV trays in plastic bags or seal them with plastic wrap and store in the freezer.

CHAPTER 20

And in Closing

Why Don't They?

Teach self-esteem building classes to grade school children. This would strengthen their self-image at a very impressionable age and save much self-inflicted doubt and criticism.

Teach classes in nutrition to high school girls. After all, they are the next meal planners of America. If they knew the importance of eating the right foods it could make a major impact on the good health of future generations.

Harness the great ocean tides for use as electricity.

Fight the drug war from the bottom up. Hold each "user" until his drug source is known. Incarcerate the dealer and hold him until his source is known. Continue this method to the top.

Build prisons and other military installations on low cost land instead of on prime waterfront property.

Treat bank customers like valued customers, the way they do at saving and loan institutions, instead of like criminals, the way they do at some banks.

Reshow prime time television during the late night and early morning hours for night workers. It could be called Prime Time Two.

Shampoo, or at least rinse hair after it has been cut, not before. No one wants to take home all those irritating clippings from the beauty or barber shop.

Provide re-closable bags in cereal and cracker containers—These items have become outrageously expensive. The least the manufacturers can do is help the product stay fresh!

Furnish super market produce plastic bags without print.—(Except for opening directions and warning for children. The green, red, or purple print rubs off on the refrigerator crisper, or on anything it touches where moisture is involved. Grocery shoppers are smart enough to know what the bags are for without printing to tell them.

Sell lean chickens instead of fat-laden ones. The consumer seems to be subsidizing the chicken rancher by paying more for waste. The buyer also must spend time removing fat or taking the chance of jeopardizing his or her health.

Stack soup alphabetically on super market shelves. It would be a real time saver.

Manufacture more white electrical cords on lamps and appliances so they will be less conspicuous. You do not see many black or brown walls!

Make cleaning containers with plastic bottoms instead of metal to prevent rust marks under the sink.

Pet Peeves

One of the nice things about writing a book is that one can voice one's own gripes. Here are some of mine:

Drivers who do not pull fully into the intersection when making a left hand turn. These are usually the same drivers who do not signal until they are ready to turn, or veer to the left when turning right.

Drivers who think signaling automatically gives them the right-of-way. They pull right out to change lanes without seeing who is already there. It is like someone who has no money in the bank, but continues to write checks, just because there are checks remaining in the book. However, with the car there is more at stake.

Pedestrians who amble across busy streets, making little power plays. Also the pedestrians who do not

at least nod or smile a "thank you" to the driver for
giving them the right-of-way.

Companies that use telephone numbers with
"clever" letters—example: FOR HELP or 777 SAVE. It
slows the dialing process while one is hunting for the
letters. Some companies are considerate and also give
numbers as well as letters.

Smokers who light up within breathing distance of
children, sometimes their own offspring!

Index

Do a Friend a Favor—
Order MY HOUSEFUL OF HINTS as a gift
Use the convenient order forms below

Send to: CRAB COVE BOOKS   Phone: (510) 945-0854
           P.O. Box 2015
           Walnut Creek, CA 94595

Please enclose $12.00 plus $1.50 shipping and handling for each book ordered. California residents add applicable state sales tax.

☐ Please send me _____ copies of MY HOUSEFUL OF HINTS.
I am enclosing $_____ (check or money order, no C.O.D.'s).

Name _____

Address _____

City _____

State _____ ZIP _____

Allow 4 to 6 weeks for delivery. Price is subject to change without notice.

Send to: CRAB COVE BOOKS   Phone: (510) 945-0854
           P.O. Box 2015
           Walnut Creek, CA 94595

Please enclose $12.00 plus $1.50 shipping and handling for each book ordered. California residents add applicable state sales tax.

☐ Please send me _____ copies of MY HOUSEFUL OF HINTS.
I am enclosing $_____ (check or money order, no C.O.D.'s).

Name _____

Address _____

City _____

State _____ ZIP _____

Allow 4 to 6 weeks for delivery. Price is subject to change without notice.